MONEY AND BITCOIN

AN VIRTUAL TRANSACTIONS TECHNOLOGY

DIPALI JADAV & MANOJ KAMBER

To our readers,

We would like to dedicate this book, Bitcoin And Money, to all those who are interested in understanding the rapidly evolving world of cryptocurrencies and their impact on the global financial system.

Our journey in exploring this topic began several years ago, when Bitcoin was still a relatively unknown concept to most people. We were fascinated by the idea of a decentralized digital currency that could potentially disrupt the traditional banking system, and we wanted to learn more.

As we delved deeper into the world of cryptocurrencies, we realized that there was a lot of confusion and misinformation surrounding this topic. Many people were skeptical of Bitcoin and other cryptocurrencies, viewing them as a speculative bubble or a tool for illegal activities.

However, we saw the potential for these digital assets to transform the way we think about money and financial transactions. We recognized that Bitcoin was not just a currency, but a technology that could enable peer-to-peer transactions without the need for intermediaries.

Through our research and analysis, we have sought to provide a clear and unbiased understanding of cryptocurrencies and their underlying technology. We have explored the history of money and the challenges faced by the current financial system, as well as the potential benefits and risks of cryptocurrencies.

We have also examined the regulatory landscape and the efforts by governments around the world to develop policies that balance innovation and consumer protection.

Our hope is that this book will serve as a comprehensive guide for anyone interested in learning about cryptocurrencies, from beginners to experts. We believe that understanding this topic is essential for anyone who wants to stay informed about the future of money and the global economy.

We would like to thank our families and loved ones for their unwavering support throughout this project. We would also like to express our gratitude to our colleagues and peers in the fields of economics and finance, whose insights and feedback have helped to shape our thinking.

Finally, we would like to thank our readers for their interest in this topic and for taking the time to explore it with us. We hope that this book will provide valuable insights and spark further discussions about the future of money and financial transactions.

Sincerely,

Dipali Jadav and Manoj Kamber

Contents

Foreword

Bitcoin and other cryptocurrencies have become some of the most talked-about topics in the world of finance and technology in recent years. As these digital assets have gained in popularity and visibility, they have raised many questions about their potential to transform the way we think about money, payments, and financial systems.

In this book, Dipali Jadav and Manoj Kamber provide a comprehensive and accessible introduction to the world of cryptocurrencies, with a particular focus on Bitcoin. They explore the history, technology, and economics of cryptocurrencies, and examine their potential implications for the future of money and finance.

What makes this book unique is its balanced and objective approach to the topic. Rather than offering a one-sided view of cryptocurrencies as either a panacea or a threat, the authors present a nuanced and thoughtful analysis of their benefits and risks. They consider both the potential opportunities and the potential challenges of cryptocurrencies, and offer a sober assessment of their role in the global financial system.

As a scholar of finance and economics, I am impressed by the depth of research and analysis that has gone into this book. The authors have drawn on a wide range of sources, including academic research, industry reports, and interviews with experts in the field. They have also synthesized this information into a clear and engaging narrative that is accessible to readers from a range of backgrounds.

I believe that this book will be of great value to anyone who is interested in understanding the world of cryptocurrencies, from students and scholars to practitioners and policymakers. It provides a thoughtful and informed perspective on a topic that is shaping the future of money and finance, and offers insights into the opportunities and challenges that lie ahead. I would like to commend Dipali Jadav and Manoj Kamber for their thoughtful and insightful analysis of this important topic, and I look forward to seeing the impact that this book will have on the broader conversation about the future of money and finance.

Preface

Blockchain technology has emerged as a revolutionary concept that has the potential to transform the way we live, work and conduct business. It has disrupted multiple industries and has the potential to create new business models and opportunities.

In this book, we will explore the basics of blockchain technology and its various applications. We will delve into the history and evolution of blockchain, starting with the creation of Bitcoin in 2009. We will then examine the different types of blockchains and their unique features. We will also discuss the various consensus mechanisms that are used to validate transactions on the blockchain.

Blockchain technology is still in its infancy, but it has already shown immense potential in various fields. We will explore the potential of blockchain beyond cryptocurrency. Blockchain technology can be used to create secure and transparent supply chains, to manage digital identities, to create decentralized autonomous organizations, and much more. We will discuss the potential of blockchain to transform industries such as finance, healthcare, real estate, and logistics. We will also explore the potential of blockchain to drive social change and create a more inclusive and equitable world.

In this book, we aim to provide a comprehensive understanding of blockchain technology. We will explain complex concepts in a simple and accessible way, using real-world examples to illustrate our points. We will also discuss the challenges and limitations of blockchain technology and the potential solutions that can help overcome these challenges.

This book is aimed at readers who are new to blockchain technology but are interested in learning more. However, it will also be useful for professionals who want to gain a deeper understanding of blockchain technology and its potential applications. Whether you are a student, an entrepreneur, or an investor, this book will provide you with the knowledge and insights you need to navigate the world of blockchain.

We hope that this book will inspire readers to explore the potential of blockchain technology and to think creatively about how it can be used to solve real-world problems. Blockchain technology has the potential to create a more secure, transparent and efficient world, and we are excited to be at the forefront of this revolution.

Acknowledgements

We would like to take this opportunity to express our deepest gratitude to the many individuals and organizations who have supported us in the creation of this book, Bitcoin And Money.

First and foremost, we would like to thank our families for their unwavering support and encouragement throughout this journey. We are grateful for their patience, understanding, and love, which have sustained us during the long hours of research and writing.

We would also like to express our sincere appreciation to our colleagues and peers in the fields of economics and finance, whose insights and feedback have been invaluable in shaping our thinking and approach to this topic. We are grateful for their willingness to engage in thoughtful discussions and debates, which have challenged and strengthened our ideas.

We are also deeply indebted to the many experts and thought leaders in the cryptocurrency community who have generously shared their knowledge and expertise with us. Their contributions have been instrumental in helping us understand the complexities and nuances of this rapidly evolving field.

We would like to extend our thanks to the publishers and editors who have supported us throughout the writing and editing process. Their guidance, expertise, and attention to detail have been instrumental in shaping this book into its final form.

We would also like to acknowledge the many students, readers, and reviewers who have provided us with valuable feedback and comments on earlier drafts of this book. Your insights and suggestions have helped us improve the clarity and relevance of our arguments.

Finally, we would like to express our appreciation to all those who have supported us in this endeavor, including our friends, mentors, and supporters in the broader academic and research communities. Your encouragement and support have been invaluable in helping us to achieve our goals.

We dedicate this book to all those who are committed to advancing knowledge and understanding in the fields of economics, finance, and technology. We hope that it will contribute to a deeper and more nuanced understanding of the opportunities and challenges posed by cryptocurrencies.

Prologue

The world of money and finance is undergoing a profound transformation. For centuries, the global economy has been built on a foundation of fiat currency, central banking, and traditional financial institutions. But in recent years, a new type of digital currency has emerged, one that is decentralized, open-source, and operates outside of the traditional financial system. This currency is known as Bitcoin, and it is just the tip of the iceberg of a larger movement towards decentralized finance.

The rise of Bitcoin has sparked a global conversation about the nature of money, the future of finance, and the role of technology in shaping our economic systems. Some see it as a revolutionary force that has the potential to disrupt traditional financial institutions and democratize access to financial services. Others view it as a speculative bubble that is fueled by hype and irrational exuberance.

In writing this book, our goal is to provide a comprehensive and objective analysis of Bitcoin and the broader cryptocurrency landscape. We seek to answer the questions that many people have about these digital assets, including what they are, how they work, and what implications they may have for the future of money and finance.

Our journey began several years ago, when Bitcoin was still a relatively unknown concept to most people. Since then, we have spent countless hours researching, analyzing, and debating the various aspects of this emerging technology. We have explored its history, its underlying technology, its potential benefits and risks, and its regulatory landscape.

We have also interviewed experts and thought leaders in the field of cryptocurrency, and sought to understand their perspectives on this rapidly evolving landscape. Through this process, we have gained a deeper appreciation for the complexities and nuances of this topic, as well as its potential to transform the way we think about money and finance.

We believe that Bitcoin and other cryptocurrencies represent a major milestone in the evolution of money and finance. They challenge many of the assumptions that underpin our current financial system, and offer a vision of a more open, transparent, and decentralized financial future. But they also raise important questions about regulation, security, and the balance of power in the financial system.

Our hope is that this book will provide a clear and balanced introduction to the world of cryptocurrencies, and stimulate further discussion and debate on this important topic. We welcome feedback and comments from readers, and look forward to engaging in a broader conversation about the future of money and finance.

CHAPTER I

Bitcoin and the Concept of Money

Bitcoin was created determined to make another sort of financial unit. As we will show over this book, the potential utilizations of Bitcoin innovation stretch out a long ways past that of a money related unit. In any case, to get a handle on the extraordinary highlights of Bitcoin innovation, one should be enough familiar with the underlying foundations of Bitcoin and in this manner with the subject of cash. In current financial hypothesis, cash is portrayed as memory. The beginning of this definition comes from the perception that individuals offer each other courtesies consistently without being responded. For instance, "gifts" of this sort are traded inside the family, among companions, or at work among partners. Undertaking housework at home, tolerating an unwanted assignment at the workplace, or giving the following supper greeting to companions are a couple of instances of such way of behaving. Consistently, we go into many such gift-giving relationships. The component that portrays these connections is that every one of the people in question keep a record of their ongoing obligation. The records are not kept recorded as a hard copy; all things being equal, they are kept in the subliminal record of the members' memory. Regardless, every member has a harsh thought regarding whether the trades of gifts also, favors are roughly adjusted. On the off chance that, in a family relationship, errands are constantly done by one individual, and the other individual benefits from this work without completing different assignments, this will cause problematic contentions that undermine the relationship. In an office, if a similar individual is constantly passed on to complete the group's evil errands, this will likewise prompt contentions. If supper solicitations in a companionship are extremely uneven, the invitee will be viewed as narrow minded, what's more, the fellowship will be undermined.

For an arrangement of gift-providing for capability, there should be a component for arriving at agreement. Understanding is typically reached when the members talk together and settle their disparities. By and by, we see that the trading of gifts and favors works flawlessly where the members realize each other well and the gathering is little. In huge gatherings, or in bunches where members are mysterious, the framework will in general break down, since it becomes hard to arrive at agreement. In such gatherings, gift-giving is supplanted by the trading of cash. Cash usurps the job of memory in complex social orders with convoluted exchanging connections. Cash keeps a record of the worldwide exchange favors. Cash is memory. An installments framework controls how its cash is addressed, the way things are created, and how the exchange of responsibility for units happens. To acquire a superior comprehension of how the Bitcoin framework works, it is beneficial to investigate customary installment frameworks. Allow us to begin by taking a gander at cash; that is, coins and banknotes. Coins and banknotes are actual items. This enjoys an incredible benefit, as the possession privileges are in every case obviously characterized. The responsibility for banknote or a coin is moved as installment from the purchaser to the vender of a decent. This permits individuals who don't have the foggiest idea about one another to exchange secretly with each another.

Further, any specialist can partake in a money installment framework; it's not possible for anyone to be rejected. There is a permissionless admittance to it. Cash has a significant hindrance since it requires the actual vicinity of the purchaser furthermore, the merchant. This limitation has become especially obvious with the ascent of the web. Likewise, it is unappealing to hold bigger amounts of money because of security and cost. Thus, supplanting actual money with computerized cash soon arisen. In a gullible execution, a purchaser would send a computerized coin to a dealer in the type of a text document. The issue is that this advanced coin can be duplicated any number of times. A purchaser could subsequently send similar computerized coin to a few venders or even hold extra duplicates of the coin. This "duplicate" situation is alluded to in the writing as the twofold spending issue. Two arrangements exist for this issue. The principal arrangement comprises in an organization being named to screen all electronic installments. This includes, specifically, checking that a purchaser legitimately owns the advanced coins that will be utilized to pay for a long term benefit. Around the world, the predominant electronic installment frameworks depend on the principal arrangement. Clients of these installment frameworks pay with electronic cash, which is likewise called store cash, bank cash, or book cash. Electronic cash is virtual cash since it doesn't exist in an actual structure. It has been made by business banks, which are liable for exact accounting. It consequently relies upon a focal power. The Bitcoin framework gives the subsequent arrangement, as it takes care of the issue of twofold spends without a focal power. To guarantee that this framework capabilities, there is a component that lays out agreement and is basically the same as the trade of favors among relatives, companions, and associates. Rather than the basic abstract agreement rules overseeing gift-giving, the Bitcoin framework ensures a goal, around the world certain agreement with the goal that anytime, the property privileges related with each Bitcoin unit are solidly settled. Consequently, the Bitcoin framework satisfies the capability of memory in complex social orders however needs no focal position to oversee it. To completely comprehend the worth of a digital currency, for example, Bitcoin, we should first grasp financial hypothesis. The remainder of this part will give a comprehension of the essentials of financial theory.We will talk about the job of cash for an economy furthermore, break down the parts of worth of a money related unit.We will then recognize the various sorts ofmoney and concentrate on their fundamental attributes and control structures. This data will assist with setting the stage to comprehend how digital currencies like Bitcoin are an extreme takeoff from existing money related instruments, which we will examine in more detail in section.

The financial hypothesis of CarlMenger recommends thatmoney may advance without government intercession. He recommended that a money related unit arises suddenly from a cycle where a decent that is regularly exchanged gradually turns into a for the most part acknowledged vehicle of trade. Such a social coordination requires no formal direction or official choices yet can rather be actuated by request that as of now exists. Further, there are solid organization impacts. The more market members there are who utilize a particular mechanism of trade, the more noteworthy is the utility that this medium offers; that is, the predominance of the mode of trade has a self-building up impact. It tends to be accepted that early financial units started along these lines. In various districts and in various times, different products and deliberations have been utilized as cash. Large numbers of these early models share a similar component: they filled in as an essential staple or on the other hand as a (stylized) thing of gems, producing a consistent demand. Albeit this is definitely not a complete show, a few instances of this incorporate stones, domesticated animals, whales' teeth, shells, and plumes. Financial units satisfy three capabilities. As a mechanism of trade, they work with exchange and work on the allotment of labor and products. As a unit of account, they act as a general reference and improve on the similar valuation of Amedium of trade is irreplaceable in amodern economy epitomized by the specialization of work; that is, when monetary entertainers practice and just produce a little subset of merchandise. Such specialization is just conceivable in the event that any remaining merchandise can be procured through exchange thus an economy with division of work should essentially be a trade economy.

A unit of record permits the upsides of all labor and products to be communicated in units of a similar reference scale and to be looked at. How much data required for a complete outline of the market is consequently considerably decreased. All things being equal of having to powerfully change the separate proportions of n(n−1) 2 sets of tradable merchandise, a unit of record gives a widespread reference to assessing various kinds of products what's more, administrations. When the costs for all labor and products are communicated in money related units, then only one single financial trade esteem is required per great (that is, n−1). This disentanglement ensuresmore straightforwardness on the lookout and lessens the inquiry and exchange expenses of exchanging. Most frequently, money related units consolidate the elements of a mode of trade and a unit of record. These two capabilities, in any case, can be handily isolated In many economies, the vehicle of trade expects the capability of a unit of record. This isn't generally the situation, as shown by the accompanying models. In the Medieval times, the variety of coins and the ceaseless changes in their valuable metal contenta prompted pounds, shillings, and pence being utilized as units of record, where a pound compared to 20 shillings or 240 pence. This made it conceivable to utilize an all inclusive cost and assess the progressions in worth of a particular coin without changing the
expressed costs of merchandise. There are still models today of situations where the capability of a unit of record is parted off from the mechanism of trade. The Unidad de Fomento in Chile (CLF) is an inflationadjusted public cost record that is resolved opposite the public money (peso) and is distributed consistently. The shopping costs in Chile are communicated in CLF. This maintains a strategic distance from the authoritative cost of making cost changes when the peso deteriorates. To work out the peso's cost, specialists just have to apply a solitary conversion standard.

In an economy that doesn't utilize cash, labor and products must be purchased through barter. An individual who claims a portion of bread however who might like to consume a container of milk would in this way initially need to find an individual who possesses a container of milk and would like to consume a portion of bread. Really at that time will the two players be willing and capable to exchange products. Therefore, a basic understanding isn't adequate. A bargain exchange must be closed assuming one party has what the other party needs as well as the other way around. This issue, referred to in the writing as the two fold occurrence of needs, makes it hard to find a reasonable exchange accomplice. Another blocking factor is the dynamic number of potential sets of tradable products. Given an inconsistent number n of various labor and products, there will be $n(n-1) 2$ various sets of tradable products. In economies which have a moderate number of various labor and products, direct deal is probably going to have a couple of hindrances. When a financial framework is more perplexing, it will comprise of millions of subjects, merchandise, and administrations. The quest for reasonable exchange accomplices (or a particular sets of tradable merchandise) will then involve extensive costs. In the event that, in any case, one great is acknowledged by all individuals from the economy, all exchanges can be settled involving this great as a vehicle of trade. A basic fortuitous event of needs is adequate for the exchange, and in this manner the quantity of pertinent sets of tradable merchandise is quickly diminished by the element n so that just $n-1$ likely sets of products remain. the quantity of potential sets of tradable merchandise in the economy with furthermore, without utilizing cash. It shows how the quantity of expected sets of tradable products floods when the quantity of merchandise increments.

- Store of Value:The store of significant worth capability of cash empowers specialists to self-safeguard against liquidity shocks. This grants utilization smoothing and insurance against surprising costs. A mechanism of trade is dependably a store of significant worth since there is a stretch of time between getting cash and spending it. Interestingly, there are numerous resources that are utilized to store investment funds, for example, gold or land, which are not utilized as amedium of trade.

To satisfy the three elements of cash introduced in segment, financial units must be storable, adaptable, separable, homogeneous, certain, scant, and cost stable. Storability. The financial unit's utilization as a mechanism of trade and a store of significant worth is contingent upon its storability. Transitory or delicate merchandise are not appropriate. The equivalent applies to merchandise that are challenging to store and thus create high capacity costs.

Adaptability. For an item to be utilized as a mechanism of trade or a store of significant worth, it should be feasible to move the property freedoms to it without significant obstacles or then again costs.

Detachability. The vehicle of trade capability requests that the financial unit (of a partial measure of it)may be traded for any picked amount of labor and products. Subsequently, cash should either be distinct or accessible in adequately little sections. Unified cash brings sizable shortcomings into an economy.

Homogeneity. Money related units (with a similar ostensible worth) should be homogeneous; that is, fungible and replaceable. Nonhomogeneous products must be exclusively assessed each time they are exchanged, which involves high exchange costs and a disappointment to work as a mode of trade.

Certainty. Both the capability of a mechanism of trade and that of a store of significant worth expect that the genuineness of the units can be confirmed and possible fakes recognized.

Shortage. A money related unit's restricted accessibility is a fundamental property for involving it as a vehicle of trade. In the event that a financial unit is accessible in limitless amounts, it will have no worth.

Solidness of significant worth. Store of significant worth and unit of record rely upon a specific cost solidness of the financial unit. Merchandise with high occasional and irregular inventory vacillations (e.g., rural items) are not reasonable.

Monetary Value: The market worth of a money related unit depends on three parts: the inherent worth, the worth of a connected commitment of installment, and a liquidity premium. The characteristic worth connects with the material, inborn worth of the item. This worth comes from the utility that outcomes from the utilization or responsibility for great or on the other hand its value as a variable of creation. The characteristic worth of a financial unit is autonomous of the money related capability of the article. A commitment of installment is a part of significant worth that isn't substantially implanted in the financial unit. As opposed to the characteristic worth, this part of significant worth is dependent upon the guarantor risk. In the event that the guarantor of the commitment doesn't satisfy his commitment, then this worth part becomes void.

Commidity Money: Product cash has an inborn worth and frequently contains a liquidity premium. The

market valuemay be higher than the inherent worth because of the liquidity premium. The inherent worth remaining parts on the off chance that the great loses its capability as a mode of trade since for this situation, the great might be consumed or might be utilized as an element of creation. The accompanying things are instances of items utilized as product cash: shells in Africa and China, rings and bits of adornments in New Guinea, and articles of clothing (furs) in North America as well as metal cash in numerous different districts of the world. Steers and fundamental groceries have frequently additionally been utilized as ware cash.

Credit Cash/Money:

Credit cash is a commitment of installment and has no inborn worth. By and large, it is a piece of paper or a computerized record which expresses that the backer will make an installment at a particular future date. This sort of commitment of installment is called an IOU (I owe you). Essentially, commitments of installment might have quite a few structures; for instance, "I owe individual × a cow on July 1, 2090" or "I owe individual × a sled ride on January 30, 2030." Most frequently, the responsibility is communicated in the common unit of account. Default risk assumes a significant part in deciding the market worth of the guaranteed installment. In such manner, the standing of the backer must be considered since a commitment to convey one ounce of gold made by individual A may have something else entirely market esteem from a similar commitment made by individual B. A commitment of installment becomesmoney when it is by and large acknowledged in exchange. Deepest nations, bank stores, which are liabilities of the individual store taking bank, are utilized for making electronic installments. A bank store isn't anything other than a commitment made by a business bank that it will trade the store for officially sanctioned cash (banknotes and coins) whenever (without hesitation). Early instances of paper cash were like different commitments of installment since they were gotten by a genuine resource (generally gold). These notes bore a promise of convertibility into a formerly concurred measure of valuable metal or into different wares. The credit character of these bills turns out to be especially clear when their starting point is thought of. The first banknotes/bills started in China during the Tang Line (the years 618-907) as a credit arrangement between confidential people. Contingent upon the standing and the reliability of the guarantor, this bill could circle and act as a money related substitute for the Kai Yuan bronze-coin chains. Undifferentiated from different sorts of cash, credit cash may likewise incorporate a liquidity premium. The liquidity premium can cause the market worth of the credit cash to be higher than the market worth of the related commitment of installment.

Flat Money:

The adage "government issued currency" gets from the Latin expression fiat (let there be), delineating that government issued currency has neither characteristic worth nor a commitment of installment and that its esteem in this manner has no key premise: it emerges from nothing (let there be cash). Its worth to be sure gets from its liquidity premium alone, and in the event that it fails to have a money related capability, its worth can tumble to nothing. Monetary standards, like the US dollar, the euro, or the Swiss franc, have a place with the class of government issued currency. The banknotes can nor be consumed nor coordinated in a creation process, nor are they gotten by gold or some other essentially significant great. The solidness of the cash's worth is ensured exceptionally by the national banks, which have an select right to give the money and the legitimate obligation to guarantee its worth remaining parts stable. In Switzerland and in numerous different nations, banknotes, and partially too coins, are legitimate delicate. Article 3 of the Government Follow up on Cash and Installment Instruments (CPIA) specifies an "commitment to acknowledge"; that is, "everybody should acknowledge Swiss banknotes in installment without limitation." This lawful premise guarantees that there is a interest for Swiss banknotes and that it advances the liquidity premium of the Swiss financial unit. Further, state backing can stabilizingly affect an on a very basic level exceptionally unpredictable class of cash. Government issued currency is a somewhat youthful peculiarity. Up until the 1970s, paper cash was upheld by gold, either verifiably or expressly, and along these lines addressed credit cash. Nonetheless, inferable from its deficiency of gold support and the irrelevant material inborn worth of a paper charge, the class of government issued currency emerged. As we will see later, Bitcoin additionally has a place to this classification.

Money Control Structure:

Financial units show different control structures, which can be generally caught by three aspects: creation, portrayal, and exchange handling. The expression "cash creation" alludes to the cycle by which new financial units can be created. The expression "portrayal" connects with whether the worth of a financial unit is attached to an actual item or whether the unit is exchanged exclusively as a virtual deliberation. The expression "exchange handling" connects with whether the transmission of a financial unit can be handled on an autonomous, decentralized premise or whether this should be done by a focal power. For cash to be significant, its amount should be scant. Shortage is generally accomplished by method for the cash creation process, which can occur under one or the other contest or on the other hand syndication. In a serious structure of cash creation, each monetary subject can make new financial units. Each individual surveys based on unadulterated personal responsibility whether delivering another money related unit, given the related production is beneficial, costs.

A financial subject will have an impetus to create another money related unit up until the place where the creation expenses of an extra unit (minimal expenses) compare to the ongoing business sector cost for that financial unit (negligible income); in different words, creation will be gone on the length of the creation interaction conveys a positive return. Cutthroat cash creation requires an innovative limitation that brings the creation process into harmony. A presents an outline of this relationship and imagines the harmony, which is arranged at the crossing point of themarginal cost and The minimal expense of creating banknotes are little, and consequently, a fake limitation must be laid out by consuming the option to make cash. Regularly, a state-controlled organization is granted the selective right to issue and deal with the public money. It is additionally feasible for this restraining infrastructure right to be privatized. The restraining infrastructure right to make cash permits the creation expenses to be kept lower than the market cost. Consumed cash creation is outlined. The cash giving monopolist picks the all out supply, and the market cost of the money related still up in the air by total interest. Cornered cash creation takes into consideration a money related unit with a positive market esteem in any event, when the minor creation costs are zero. An illustrative illustration of monopolistic cash creation is the development of the actual Swiss franc. The Swiss Public Bank has the select right to give banknotes what's more, consequently has an imposing business model over the making of money. The expense of overall, to thirty pennies (called "Rappen").

For the 100 franc note, the expense is just 0.3 percent of its fairly estimated worth. Under ideal rivalry in the creation of cash, the market would be overflowed with banknotes until the genuine worth of a note rose to the expense of creating it. This too really intends that undeniably more assets would need to be surrendered to create a given complete worth for the vehicle of trade. From a cultural perspective, this prompts a wasteful allotment of assets and an effectiveness advantage for the monopolistic cash giving process.

Notwithstanding the referenced proficiency contemplations, there is a further significant distinction among cutthroat and monopolistic cash creation. Under rivalry, the cash not entirely set in stone by creation expenses and total interest. Conversely, a restraining infrastructure guarantor can effectively impact the cash supply and answer changes sought after. Since monetary exercises are frequently of a repeating nature, a cash giving monopolistic foundation has the ability to balance out the worth of cash by extending or on the other hand getting the cash supply. National banks are making new cash by giving credits to business banks or purchasing unfamiliar trade and protections. At the point when a national bank gives a credit to a business bank, the credit is displayed on the resources side of its accounting report. Interestingly, the recently made cash is set up for the liabilities side of its asset report. This interaction is called balance sheet augmentation. Since the recently made cash is possibly circling in the economy, new "cash" has been made through this accounting report expansion. In the business bank's monetary record, the advance is displayed on the liabilities side and the recently made cas on the resources side. Furnishing a national manage an account with the optional influence to supply change the cash to settle the value level can be of incredible advantage to society.

In any case, a serious level of trust should be set in any imposing business model provider of cash. If the autonomy of the establishment isn't ensured, the restrictive right to make cash can prompt harmful funding of public consumption through the "print machine," which has frequently come about in the total obliteration of the particular cash. Money related history covers various instances of such cases (see box 1.6 and box 1.7). presentation the genuine worth of cash for different monetary standards from 1960 until 2018. Consider, for instance, the way for the genuine worth of cash for the Argentinian peso. In this chart we have standardized the genuine worth of cash to one in 1960. This implies that one Argentinian peso could get one unit of a normalized bushel of labor and products around then. Around seventeen years after the fact, a similar unit of cash would purchase just 0.0001 units of similar normalized bushel of merchandise and wares. Approximately thirty years after the fact, one Argentinien peso would purchase 0.0000000000001 units.

The value history of the Argentinian peso isn't an exception. It would be troublesome, truth be told to find an emerging nation that has not encountered an obliteration of the genuine worth of its cash over the most recent sixty years. Further, figure 1.6 demonstrates the way that in any event, for fostered The present financial request can't be depicted by a simply cornered moneycreation process.

Business banks make bank stores which, albeit not legitimate delicate, are generally speaking thought about what could be compared to legitimate delicate and are flowed in a similarmanner. Bank stores aren't anything else than commitments of the individual business bank to reclaim the lawful delicate on request. For instance, in the event that an individual has a US$100 banknote, the person is in control of the lawful delicate. Be that as it may, if a similar individual has a store account with a business keep money with a surplus of US$100, the total is a commitment of installment — as such, acknowledge cash as depicted in segment 1.4.2. Business banks make cash likewise to the national banks. Business banks produce cash (i.e., request stores) when they issue credits to confidential people and organizations. At the point when business banks issue credits to their clients, they increment the clients' interest stores and book the credits as their clients' liabilities. In fact, a business bank can make any measure of cash (request stores) by conceding advances.

By and by, the benefit of this business limitsmoney creation. In expansion, there areminimum saves and other administrative limitations that limit private cash creation. Nor is it in the bank's revenue to spur so that's what many interest stores it can't keep the guarantee to trade them for lawful delicate. For this situation, the bank would become illiquid. The possibility of business bank illiquidity has encouraged numerous monetary emergencies before and is one of the primary purposes behind the thorough guideline of monetary notwithstanding the gamble engaged with fragmentary hold banking, the significance of request stores for installments ought not be underestimated. In numerous nations, request stores are the main choice that people need to hold and move cash in a virtual form. In spite of the fact that there is no legitimate commitment to acknowledge private cash, electronic moves and card installments are universal to the point that acknowledgment is boundless. Hence, a great many people expect erroneously that request stores are national bank cash.

This bogus supposition that is advanced by the at-standard exchanging of interest stores also, national bank cash in ordinary times. In the event that a business bank is presently not in the position to satisfy its guarantee to convey national bank cash on request, just bank clients will see the distinction between national bank cash and business interest stores. There are two different ways that cash can be addressed — financial units either can have a actual portrayal or can have a virtual portrayal. Actual financial units are connected to an article. The actual control of the article additionally infers ownership of the relating esteem. For instance, on the off chance that somebody controls a actual gold coin, then, at that point, he fundamentally has the privilege to utilize it. Actual money related units are especially alluring a direct result of their basic dealing with. Since the holder of an actual financial unit is consequently the proprietor of the comparing esteem, the proprietorship privileges to the units, which are flowing uninhibitedly in the economy, are in every case obviously characterized without anybody keeping records.

This component takes into consideration a decentralized installment framework where actual financial units can change hands between specialists without the inclusion of an outsider. Consequently, actual financial units permit specialists to stay unknown and safeguard the proprietor against fundamental conditions since the exchange of the unit of significant worth does not need any extra foundation or trust. Actual money related units have a few inconveniences, which arc portrayed beneath. Confined to a geographic area. Actual money related units are restricted to exchanges in which the gatherings (or agents) stand eye to eye to make the trade. Care and transport. Cash in actual structure produces expenses of supervision what's more, transport. The financial units must be expertly put away, got and frequently guaranteed. A huge part of these expenses are straightforwardly connected with the overall actual mass of the put away sums as well as the distance of a vehicle. Actual trustworthiness. Whether or not cash creation is cutthroat or hoarded, the financial unit should be impervious to fraud. With cornered cash creation, it is important to guarantee that the financial units would be able just be created by the committed syndication. Under rivalry, it is important to guarantee that items with comparative appearance and lower creation costs are forestalled from entering course as cash substitutes. The honesty of a physical money related unit is frequently ensured by putting security highlights on them. Section and detachability. Actual financial units are not completely detachable.

Partitioning an actual money related unit can be costly (valuable metals) or inconceivable (banknotes). Government issued currency frameworks make various groups, and national banks ensure, for instance, that a banknote with the number 100 imprinted on it is traded for ten banknotes which have the number 10 imprinted on them. Virtual cash is an option in contrast to cash in actual structure. Virtual financial units incorporate a wide range of financial units that don't have an actual portrayal. More definitively, a money related unit is virtual in the event that it tends to be moved to another proprietor without the move including an adjustment of command over an actual item.

Virtual cash shares many ascribes of actual cash without the drawbacks of an actual portrayal, however there are likewise disadvantages. While the responsibility for actual article is obviously settled by the whereabouts of the comparing object, responsibility for virtual case is contestable. To balance this issue, the legitimization furthermore, confirmation of virtual cases happens by means of implied or unequivocal records that keep a record of all monetary subjects' property A credulous endeavor to address esteem for all intents and purposes is use "cash" information documents. This sort of information record could be utilized as a computerized banknote and flow uninhibitedly in a way undifferentiated from to actual banknotes. However long the responsibility for information document can be obviously demonstrated, no record is vital. This thought, notwithstanding, has one significant issue. In differentiation to actual articles, virtual articles can be effortlessly replicated. Such "cash" information documents thusly come up short on generally fundamental central quality of cash, in particular shortage, and can't secure itself as cash.

Certain records are exclusively founded on the oral understanding of the members who use them and are hence restricted to little, all around arranged networks. Box arrangements with an illustration of a virtual financial unit in view of an implied record. Bigger social bunches produce complex frameworks and convoluted possession connections that make the utilization of express records necessary. For such cases, data sets are utilized to store records in composed or computerized structure. A great and extremely striking illustration of a virtual (however not computerized) cash in view of an certain record is given by the American anthropologist William Henry Furness III. Toward the start of the 20th hundred years, he spent a while on the German Micronesian island of Gab to concentrate on the Gab locals' lifestyle and culture. He was especially intrigued by the money related arrangement of the island's occupants. In his report, he composes of enormous grindstone like arrangements that were removed from the island of Palau, only 280 miles away, and afterward boated to Gab. When there, the stones were utilized as money.a

However, rather than relentlessly moving the stones — each with a measurement of up to thirteen feet — to the property of the new proprietor with every exchange, the occupants consented to leave the awkward articles at their separate spot. The main unequivocal variable was simply the local area would perceive the difference in possession. News about the exchanges that had occurred and the ensuing changes in possession would be conveyed among the island's occupants until all had been informed. Despite the fact that themillstones are actual articles, the case to their proprietorship was withdrawn from them and was exchanged freely. This separation has the outcome that actual command over the stone no longer involves responsibility for actual article's worth. As indicated by the reports of Furness, the course of virtualization was all around cutting edge, such that even the unit worth of a stone which sank in the ocean while being moved from Palau to Gab was as yet acknowledged as a mechanism of trade, regardless of whether the actual stone had been lying at the lower part of the sea for ages. The actual stones were of auxiliary significance and were not pertinent to laying out real privileges of proprietorship — this partition being the trademark as indicated by which the financial unit fulfills our definition of virtuality.

The present monetary framework depends on a multitiered design of express records. The national banks keep records of the resources of the business banks. The business banks thus keep records of their clients' resources. As we will find in the accompanying parts, Bitcoin is likewise overseen based on an express record, in particular the Bitcoin blockchain. Exchanging with actual money related units gives an extremely elevated degree of anonymity. For the most part, there are no information, or just unpleasant approximations, that show where the physical money related units are really found. Consequently, finding individual is troublesome money related units, and this is for the most part just conceivable on the off chance that the actual financial unit isn't totally homogeneous or on the other hand in the event that it has a chronic number or bears another particular element.

Frameworks with virtual financial units are substantially more straightforward. The presence of a record actually intends that somewhere around one party is constantly educated about the ongoing dispersion regarding all financial units as well as pretty much every one of the exchanges, accordingly subverting namelessness. Whether or not the record is in composed, advanced (unequivocal register) or verbal (verifiable register) structure, it is inescapable that something like one limited gathering will approach to a portion of the data connecting with the possession relationship and the executed exchanges. This reality raises specific worries about security since there may likewise be great explanations behind not uncovering installment and possession data.

Exchange Handling:

Exchange handling might be brought together or decentralized. Decentralized exchange handling implies that the holder of a financial unit can move its proprietorship freedoms freely with next to no commitment to enroll the guide of an outsider. Rather than this, with incorporated handling, a focal authority is liable for handling the exchanges, and its arrangement is required for the financial unit to be moved. Autonomous of whether exchange handling is brought together or decentralized, the three following value-based prerequisites should be satisfied.

Conditional limit. This prerequisite guarantees that exchanges can be started furthermore, esteem units moved. Conditional authenticity. This prerequisite guarantees that there is a controlmechanism to ensure that exchanges may just be started by the legitimate owner(s).

Value-based agreement. This necessity guarantees that there is an interaction which lays out an unambiguous dispersion of responsibility for money related units by any stretch of the imagination times. Actual financial units are, by definition, handled in a decentralized way. The ongoing proprietor of an actual financial unit can uninhibitedly figure out where they wish to keep the actual article and where they can thus hand it over, along with its unit esteem, to another proprietor. Every one of the three prerequisites are subsequently consequently fulfilled: the actual article can (conditional limit) just (value-based authenticity) be moved by the ongoing proprietor and is constantly possessed by the person who has command over the actual article (conditional agreement). The end of actual portrayal subverts the intrinsic value-based agreement and prompts the requirement for records. At the point when records are utilized, the topic of who ought to oversee them should be tended to. It would create significant issues in the event that each member reserved the option to deal with the record. In contrast with the model, a general right to change the record would be a plausible choice for little, very much organized gatherings, however when the framework arrives at a particular size and the installment streams become more complicated, the utilization of an implied public record would definitely set off questions about the genuine condition of the record. In addition, agitators could dissipate bogus reports by imparting controlled exchanges.

In data innovation, these issues are known as the Byzantine Commanders Most virtual money related units depend on records that utilization a concentrated arrangement of exchange handling where a predefined set of specialists is given an elite power to deal with the record. By and large, these specialists are business banks, which consequently give the fundamental installment framework. These organizations lay out an organization of branches, acknowledge composed installment arranges, and work with client-supported association through electronic correspondence channels (value-based limit). Simultaneously, they confirm the authenticity of the installment orders to guarantee that main genuine exchanges track down their direction into the record (conditional authenticity). That's what selectiveness guarantees, by any means
times, just a single form of the record exists, consequently fulfilling the prerequisite of conditional agreement. The presence of a focal power assists with streamlining the conditional cycle and accomplish agreement. Simultaneously, the foundation of such an imposing business model is helpless to the gamble of negligence. In principle, a focal authority can randomly modify the record or on the other hand will not deal with exchanges that are on a very basic level genuine. Indeed, even in states where such an unmistakable maltreatment of this position isn't normal, various inquiries should be tended to: how much ought to and may an economy become reliant upon focal infrastructures?Who settles on the distribution of the record-keeping honor, and how is it forestalled that a focal occurrence is debased or extricates syndication rents?

Likewise, a focal foundation expands the gamble of criminal assaults and seizure of assets by outsiders. Models incorporate programmer assaults; tyrannical, constrained changes of balances into recently made monetary forms; or erratic seizures of money related units. Specifically, a squeezing scholarly inquiry that should be tended to is whether the term "property" has any pertinence assuming the separate unit of significant worth is just transferrable what's more, usable subject to another element's understanding. We are confronting a quandary. From one perspective, according to an effectiveness point of view, a virtual financial unit is ideal. Then again, virtual portrayal requires brought together exchange handling with every one of the negatives portrayed previously. It would in this way be alluring to plan a virtual money related unit that highlights decentralized exchange handling. In 2008, the Bitcoin designers proposed a virtual money related that doesn't depend on unified establishments.

CHAPTER II

The Trust With Bitcoins

"We have proposed a framework for electronic exchanges without depending on trust." Subsequently starts the finishing up segment of a nine-page report presented on the Cryptography internet mailing list on Halloween 2008. Named "Bitcoin: A Shared Electronic Money Framework," the paper recorded Satoshi Nakamoto (a nom de plume) its author.1 Regardless of huge exertion, the personality of Bitcoin's maker has never been definitively determined.2 He was last heard from in 2011. Incidentally for a prophet of decentralization, the family name "Nakamoto" in Japanese signifies "of focal beginning." Whoever Satoshi was, one thing is clear: He, or she, or they, were dead wrong. Trust is key to Bitcoin, as well concerning the influx of blockchain and dispersed record arrangements following its methodology — and not for no obvious reason the words "trust" or "trusted" seem multiple times in the short paper. Bitcoin would be pointless in the event that it were not trusted. The astounding ascent in the worth of cryptographic forms of money since Bitcoin depends totally on individuals' eagerness to believe that sections on secretly worked, appropriated computerized records are essentially as genuine as cash. The many nonfinancial, blockchain-based new companies furthermore, endeavor blockchain projects lay on a comparable conviction. Appropriated record networks unite networks that in any case wouldn't confide in each other adequately. They are, as per the title of a main story in The Financial expert, "trust machines."4 Bitcoin's blockchain component very well could have sent off an upset in trust — and just in time. For a considerable length of time, the advertising firm Edelman has directed worldwide studies of confidence in government, business, and the media. Its yearly report, delivered at the World Financial Gathering yearly gathering in Davos, offers a nitty gritty depiction of cultural trust designs. The image isn't empowering. The greater part of the trust records have been on a descending pattern for some time. As of late, the disintegration of trust has sped up. The 2017 Edelman Trust Gauge report was entitled A Collapse of Trust. Just 15% of the overall public accepts "the framework" is working. The "significant emergency of trust" uncovered in the review is both profound and wide. It stretches out across all classes of organizations —

including government, the media, partnerships, also, nongovernmental associations (NGOs) — and is shared by both the informed public and the mass populace.

Other ongoing studies offer comparable discoveries, particularly in the Assembled States. Only one out of five Americans in a Seat Exploration Center survey said they confided in the public authority in 2015, a year prior to a tweaking official political race that carried that suspicion to new heights. And Americans, it appears, have zero faith in one another considerably more. As soon as 2013, only 33% of Americans said in a Related Press survey that a great many people can be relied upon, contrasted with half in 1972, when the Overall Social Review previously asked the question.8 Almost 66% — a record high — said that "you can't be as well cautious" while managing individuals. Nobody who follows recent developments wouldn't believe these measurements. The contemporary trust emergency is the finish of examples that have been producing for a long time. Two persuasive, top of the line books distributed around the turn of the thousand years, Robert Putnam's Bowling Alone furthermore, Francis Fukuyama's Trust, cautioned of the fraying of cultural trust. Utilizing a snowstorm of overviews and other examination, Putnam featured the disintegration of nearby trust networks in America, encapsulated by the decrease in bowling associations comparative with individual bowling. He saw this as a malignant turn of events that made sense of the development of social pathologies. Five years sooner, Fukuyama comparably had sounded the caution about an emergency of trust worldwide, and especially in contemporary America. Regardless of its standing for tough independence, he brought up, America really profited from undeniable levels of reliance. However, that seems, by all accounts, to be evolving. The trust emergency that journalists, for example, Fukuyama and Putnam cautioned of twenty years prior is presently a reality. The results might be desperate. We as a whole settle on choices in light of trust consistently. Would it be advisable for me I get into the secondary lounge of this vehicle? Does the bundle of fish that I need to buy harbor a dangerous infection? Do I go out on the town with this individual? Would it be advisable for me I type my credit card number into this crate on my PC screen? There are not many human associations, and less still deals, that don't depend in huge part on the characteristics of trust involved. As indicated by the humanist Niklas Luhmann, trust makes human culture itself possible. Without trust, we would have to check and get the unwavering quality of everybody we experienced.

That would be an incomprehensible assignment. Trust is the oil that greases up friendly and business cooperations and the variable that delivers the endless intricacy of the advanced world manageable. Trust, be that as it may, is in excess of a passage. It has outcomes. Trust shapes cooperations, possibly in extremely critical ways. The people who are trusted are strong. The people who are not should work harder every step of the way to acquire the certainty of others, putting them in a tough spot. Frameworks that adjust the extent of trust, hence, change social orders. Trust shapes both the macrostructures of public financial execution and the microstructures of individual and firm associations. All over the planet, high-trust social orders outflank low-trust ones. Business researchers likewise see as experimentally that organizations where trust is high perform better. Trust capabilities as friendly capital. It makes stores of altruism that work with social cooperations and deals. The abundance of society is consequently increased.

Trust began in the limited bounds of families and little nearby networks. In the advanced world, however, it is basically difficult to restrict collaborations to those circles. High-trust social orders have created societies, accepted practices, and general sets of laws that give their residents the certainty to stretch out trust to outsiders. In a high-trust climate, there is less requirement for meddling guidelines and coercive implementation since individuals are willing to act without them. The vast majority are dependable more often than not. What's more, at the point when they are not, the mix of lawful approvals and prevailing burden can address unfortunate behavior.

In monetary terms, trust diminishes exchange costs. It liberates parties from the costs of obtaining data and observing the way of behaving of those they execute with. Trust connections will generally be more adaptable than untrusted ones in light of the fact that the gatherings don't have to determine exhaustively what comprises suitable direct. That, thus, further develops execution. Nobel Prize-winning financial analyst Ronald Coase's persuasive "hypothesis of the firm" can be perceived as a reaction to the impediments of trust. Firms force progressive administration and control structures in light of the fact that in any case they can't confide in their workers or accomplices to dependably act. If there were more trust, that would permit significant new business courses of action to thrive. The sharing economy scholar Rachel Botsman accepts that is precisely what's going on today: "We are imagining a sort of trust that can make everything go smoothly of business and work with one individual to the next connections in the period of conveyed networks and cooperative marketplaces." Trust appears to be an unalloyed decent. Why, then, at that point, does Oliver Williamson, Coase's kindred financial matters Nobel laureate, proclaim it a "diffuse and disheartening idea" that delivers "no conspicuous worth added"? How could the ancestor of the blockchain approach compose, soon after the send off of his incredible innovation, "The foundational issue with customary cash is all the trust that is expected to make it work"? And how could Beam Dillinger, the cryptographer who investigated the first Bitcoin programming code, call trust "just about a profanity"? Trust is surprisingly perplexing. Assuming we wish to grasp the potential furthermore, risks of the blockchain, we should begin by inspecting the idea of trust and its appearances in the contemporary world.

Trust is one of those "I know it when I see it" ideas that, upon closer assessment, become maddeningly challenging to nail down. As the business morals researcher Larue Tone Hosmer wryly notices, "There gives off an impression of being broad settlement on the significance of confidence in human lead, yet ... a similarly inescapable absence of settlement on a reasonable meaning of the build." Throughout the course of recent many years, researchers in administration, brain science, theory, and different fields have created significant assemblages of writing on the importance of trust. This grant reveals insight into both the importance of trust and its fundamental parts. Trust isn't paired. It is what is going on where trust is completely missing. In the event that we couldn't underestimate anything without confirming it first, we would be unable to endure a day. All things considered, there are various degrees of trust. Putnam recognizes "thick" trust, emerging from affectionate social connections, from "dainty" trust, among a general public in general. Fukuyama separates high-trust and low-trust societies.25 The executives researchers Jay Barney and Check Hansen separate "solid" trust (not upheld by ensures of execution), "semi-solid" trust (where the gatherings make authorization components, yet they are dependent upon possible disappointment), and "powerless" trust (where regulation or some other instrument ensures performance). Fernando Flores and Robert Solomon separate "gullible" trust, in light of unadulterated confidence, from "valid" trust, grounded in relationships. Trust can be seen on a range along various aspects. The oversimplified meaning of trust is mental gamble appraisal: Am I legitimized in depending on this individual or association?. I trust the pilot to fly my plane securely to its objective since I realize that mishaps are very uncommon. I give my Mastercard to a waiter in an eatery since I sensibly expect to be that she won't utilize it to run up unapproved charges (and in the event that she does, my credit card organization will switch them). Oliver Williamson, the business analyst, calls this peculiarity "calculativeness" since it is dependent upon objective estimation. On the off chance that I give my vehicle keys to a valet, the likely misfortune assuming that the person in question takes my vehicle might be perfect, yet the likelihood is low, checking is simple, and change — through policing protection — will probably restore me. On the other hand, on the off chance that I am approached to wire my life reserve funds to a Nigerian sovereign I met by email, I would be advised to be quite certain about the approaching prize. While the mental aspect is significant, it can't address the whole of trust. Any other way, trust would be just judicious dependence.

This is the line among trust and confirmation. A moneylender demanding that a borrower give point by point, evaluated fiscal reports and broad insurance might be certain of reimbursement, however nobody would call that a relationship of trust. In the event that the moneylender endorses a credit to a longstanding client without documentation, it likely could be on the grounds that her data about the client and experience from earlier experiences make it a levelheaded, self-intrigued choice, not genuinely one of trust. This was Williamson's justification behind distinctive trust from calculativeness. However now and again we act in manners that mental gamble evaluation can't make sense of. Certain individuals in all actuality do answer Nigerian email tricks or loan cash to companions who they know are probably not going to reimburse it. What's more, as Fukuyama featured, paces of trust shift among social orders, proposing further social and For a long time, the advertising firm Edelman has led worldwide overviews of confidence in government, business, and the media. Its yearly report, delivered at the World Financial Gathering yearly gathering in Davos, offers a nitty gritty depiction of cultural trust designs. The image isn't empowering. The greater part of the trust files have been on a descending pattern for some time. As of late, the disintegration of trust has sped up. The 2017 Edelman Trust Indicator report was entitled A Collapse of Trust.5 Just 15% of the all inclusive community accepts "the framework" is working. The "significant emergency of trust" uncovered in the review is both profound and wide. It stretches out across all classes of organizations — including government, the media, enterprises, also, nongovernmental associations (NGOs) — and is shared by both the informed public and the mass populace. Other late reviews offer comparable discoveries, particularly in the Unified States.6 Only one out of five Americans in a Seat Exploration Center survey said they confided in the public authority in 2015, a year prior to a tweaking official political decision that carried that incredulity to new heights. And Americans, it appears, have no faith in one another considerably more. As soon as 2013, only 33% of Americans said in a Related Press survey that a great many people can be relied upon, contrasted with half in 1972, when the Overall Social Study previously asked the question.8 Almost 66% — a record high — said that "you can't be as well cautious" while managing individuals. Nobody who follows recent developments wouldn't believe these measurements. The contemporary trust emergency is the perfection of examples that have been creating for a long time.

Two powerful, top of the line books distributed around the turn of the thousand years, Robert Putnam's Bowling Alone also, Francis Fukuyama's Trust, cautioned of the fraying of cultural trust. Utilizing a snowstorm of overviews and other examination, Putnam featured the disintegration of nearby trust networks in America, encapsulated by the decrease in bowling associations
comparative with individual bowling. He saw this as a malevolent turn of events that made sense of the development of social pathologies. Five years sooner, Fukuyama correspondingly had sounded the caution about an emergency of trust worldwide, and especially in contemporary America. Regardless of its standing for tough independence, he called attention to, America really profited from undeniable levels of association. Yet, that seems, by all accounts, to be evolving. The trust emergency that separates high-trust and low-trust societies. The executives researchers Jay Barney and Check Hansen separate "solid" trust (not upheld by ensures of execution), "semi-solid" trust (where the gatherings make implementation instruments, however they are dependent upon likely disappointment), and "frail" trust (where regulation or some other component ensures performance). Fernando Flores and Robert Solomon separate "innocent" trust, in light of unadulterated confidence, from "bona fide" trust, grounded in relationships. Trust can be seen on a range along numerous aspects. The shortsighted meaning of trust is mental gamble appraisal: Am I legitimized in depending on this individual or association? I trust the pilot to fly my

plane securely to its objective since I realize that mishaps are very uncommon. I give my Visa to a waiter in a café on the grounds that I sensibly expect to be that she won't utilize it to run up unapproved charges (and assuming she does, my credit card organization will invert them). Oliver Williamson, the financial specialist, calls this peculiarity "calculativeness" since it is dependent upon levelheaded estimation. On the off chance that I give my vehicle keys to a valet, the expected misfortune assuming the person takes my vehicle might be perfect, yet the likelihood is low, checking is simple, and review — through policing protection — will probably restore me. On the other hand, on the off chance that I am approached to wire my life reserve funds to a Nigerian sovereign I met by email, I would do well to be quite sure about the approaching award. While the mental aspect is significant, it can't address the whole of trust. Any other way, trust would be just sane dependence. This is the line among trust and confirmation. A moneylender demanding that a borrower give point by point, inspected budget reports and broad insurance might be certain of reimbursement, yet nobody would call that a relationship of trust. In the event that the bank supports a credit to a longstanding client without documentation, it likely could be on the grounds that her data about the client and experience from earlier experiences make it a normal, self-intrigued choice, not genuinely one of trust. This was Williamson's justification behind distinctive trust from calculativeness. However here and there we act in manners that mental gamble evaluation can't make sense of. Certain individuals really do answer Nigerian email tricks or loan cash to companions who they know are probably not going to reimburse it. What's more, as Fukuyama featured, paces of trust shift among social orders, proposing further social and Fundamental trust breakdowns may likewise happen when connections cross such a large number of limits, whether authoritative or political. Without a typical lawful climate or business structure, the exchange expenses of laying out baselines for trust might be excessively perfect. Furthermore, trust separates when a trust stage itself is sabotaged. At the point when the credit authority Equifax conceded in September 2017 that individual data on more than 140 million Americans had been gotten to from its servers, it brought down the degree of confidence in credit and personality administrations generally. Even before that, a concentrate by the U.S. Division of Trade in 2016 had observed that close to half of Americans were hindered from utilizing internet business administrations because of safety or security concerns. Trust, hence, is a two-sided coin. On one side is a conviction established in some blend of normal and close to home variables; on the other is acknowledgment of uncontrolled gamble.

The authoritative conduct researcher Roger Mayer and his coauthors, in a much-refered to article, reviewed originations of confidence in a few trains and proposed an integrative definition: "[Trust is] the ability of a party to be powerless against the activities of one more party in view of the assumption that the other will play out a specific activity critical to the trustor, regardless of the capacity to screen or control that other part." To put it plainly, trust is sure vulnerability. The advantages of trust emerge from its capacity to invigorate what Botsman depicts as a "sure relationship to the unknown." That additionally produces costs. This Janus-confronted perspective of trust — a wellspring of solidarity as well as risk — makes sense of why the creator of the Bitcoin whitepaper thought that it is so disagreeable. There is no trust without weakness. What's more, weakness customarily implies providing up capacity to other people. You trust the bank by enabling it to control your cash. You do indeed the very same with the extortionist.

The heavenly body of plan choices that shape a framework is known as its "design." Engineering is power since it characterizes the restrictions of human collaborations. Similarly as the actual design of neighborhoods decides the personality of networks, the advanced engineering of correspondences organizations and data frameworks shapes potential open doors for development, imagination, and free articulation online. For innovations, design depicts the manners in which the parts of a framework collaborate with each other. initiate people to surrender power or control. Acknowledge authorities, for example, Experian and Equifax, for instance, employ extraordinary authority since they empower exchanges like credits. Individual moneylenders, by and large, had a lot harder time collecting the information important to survey person reliability. What gets action going in this plan is the mediators' capacity to total action on the two sides. Monetary administrations connections are a genuine illustration of mediator trust. Business banks sit in the center of the exchange stream among contributors and borrowers, creating what's more, paying interest en route. Venture banks structure and halfway monetary exchanges in capital business sectors. Monetary administrations now create about 30% of all corporate benefits in the, all of us in view of the force of such intermediation. Middle person trust is especially huge online. Promoters trust Google since it shows them straightforward evaluating and execution measurements for their promotions, while clients trust it since it returns top notch search results encompassed by promotions they see as significant. Amazon and eBay make trusted conditions for exchanges. Uber and Airbnb make markets around transportation also, dwelling, through which clients connect with outsiders in manners they never would somehow or another. They are frequently depicted as shared, yet clients are really confiding in the stage, not private connections or communitydefined administration systems. This large number of models lead to a trust compromise, in which clients surrender an opportunity to acquire the advantages of trust. In shared trust, they should notice the standards of the local area; in Leviathan trust, they are docile to the state; and in mediator trust, they get themselves into walled gardens by surrendering command over private information. Ongoing discussions about the power of online stages, for example, Google and Facebook mirror this concern. These stages control how clients see the world by molding their data abstains from food, also, they control markets through the force of intermediation. Network impacts make it challenging for contenders to sabotage their strength. This challenge will be investigated in more prominent profundity in part. The blockchain makes another sort of trust that none of the laid out models includes. Conspicuous investor and LinkedIn pioneer Reid Hoffman portrays it as "trustless trust." The expression has gotten on. In spite of the fact that it sounds self-disconnected, the two sides are significant. If digital forms of money furthermore, circulated records didn't move trust, they would come up short. However on the off chance that they accomplished trust as a substitute through legislatures or solid middle people, they wouldn't essentially contrast from the norm. On a blockchain network, nothing is thought to be dependable ... with the exception of the result of the actual organization. This particular plan characterizes the scene for the blockchain's collaborations with regulation, guideline, and administration.

In any exchange, there are three components that might be relied upon: the counterparty, the mediator, and the question goal mechanism. The blockchain attempts to supplant each of the three with programming code. Individuals are addressed through inconsistent advanced keys, which take out the context oriented factors that people use to assess dependability. The exchange stage is a disseminated machine worked by obscure members who are in it only for the cash. What's more, debate goal happens through "savvy contracts" executing predefined calculations. What makes an exchange substantial are cryptographic confirmations that the other party can check numerically. Thus the familiar saying, "in verification we trust," among bitcoin enthusiasts, in differentiation to the legend "In God We Trust" on U.S. monetary orders. Online exchanges as of now depend on encryption and algorithmic standing frameworks. Each time you purchase something from Amazon.com or use Facebook to stay aware of your companions, you are trusting a generally mechanized, softwarebased framework.

In any event, when you stick your charge card into an ATM and get cash out of an opening, you are believing a machine to do what was quintessentially human work. The significant point is why we trust the machines. We have certainty that a PC won't be moronic, or slow, or careless, or one-sided in the way that a human record-manager may be. That is PCs' specialty well: They quickly and reliably execute programs. In any case, there are things that machines generally don't do, or can't do. Blockchains accomplish more than rouse trust in the unwavering quality of their record sections. They produce a specific sort of trust that ought to be inspected in its own particular manner. Blockchain trust is theoretical. You can't see a bitcoin; it is only a bunch of exchange records on a dispersed record. However that is not really extraordinary in the present world. We acknowledge that our ledgers address genuine cash and our stock buys address genuine value, despite the fact that we view them electronically. Protected innovation privileges like copyrights, brand names, and licenses are significant wellsprings of upper hand and alienable resources in themselves.

Moreover, immaterialness is a standard issue with all online interactions.80 The more critical part of blockchain trust is that it cuts off the association between institutional entertainers and the dependable framework. To acknowledge a digital money exchange as substantial is to believe the organization it depends on, without fundamentally confiding in any singular member or higher authority. One can acknowledge the agreement of a disseminated assortment of free PCs as the genuine condition of the record. In its least difficult structure, this is the trust transformation of the blockchain and dispersed record innovation. It instills trust in aggregates of machines, while emptying it out of those machines' human bosses.

There have forever been the people who want a world free from corporate and administrative control. Driving figures in the PC upheaval were impacted by the nonconformity upsides of the 1960s. An age afterward, a large number of the people who advanced the ascent of the

Web considered it to be a way to associate individuals all over the planet straightforwardly, without the impedance of country states. The little however complex Cypherpunk development looked for specialized answers for execute this vision. It considered the Web to be evidence that even the overbearing influence of the state needed to give way to the laws of arithmetic basic cryptography and the computer programming hidden parcel exchanged information organizations. The early Sun Microsystems engineer John Gilmore broadly proclaimed that "the Net deciphers restriction as harm also, courses around it."83 The ongoing time is one in which trust in organizations and legislatures is profoundly shaken, while confidence in innovation as a power for change stays in salvageable shape. The ideal climate for a methodology apparently utilizes the last option to make the previous old. As Brian Behlendorf, leader chief of the Hyperledger open-source circulated record consortium puts it, "Blockchain innovation can permit us to carry on with work in a climate of declining trust."84 It is the suitable trust engineering for the current verifiable second. However in opposition to Reid Hoffman's exquisite manner of expression, the blockchain is not totally trustless. It might advance legitimate certainty, yet not without weakness. What Satoshi Nakamoto and the individuals who followed him made was really another sort of dependability, strong yet flawed. Blockchain trust isn't a paradoxical expression. It is an unmistakable peculiarity that should be inspected according to its own preferences. Doing the way to understanding is as well how blockchain innovation works, yet why it will succeed and where it will fizzle.

There is a notable rationale puzzle including two watches, every one of whom remains before an entryway. One entryway prompts wealth, the other to death. You should scrutinize the gatekeepers to choose the right entryway. One gatekeeper generally replies honestly; the other consistently lies. The catch: You don't realize which will be which. The riddle at first appears to be unthinkable. You won't ever know whether a response you get is honest. However there is a rich arrangement: Ask one gatekeeper which entryway the other would suggest — anything answer you get, go through the contrary entryway. The honest watchman will direct you toward the entryway of death since that is what the liar would do. The liar knows that the honest one would guide you to the entryway of wealth, so he additionally directs you toward the entryway of demise. Pick the other one. Satoshi Nakamoto tackled the riddle of computerized cash — and in this manner, fostered another trust engineering — utilizing a comparative methodology: modifying the issue. The instrument for individuals to make installments unhesitatingly with a decentralized computerized money is to pay individuals with it. Instead of treat cash as simply the result of the framework, Bitcoin involves it as an information. At the point when Satoshi posted his thoughts online in 2008, a couple of beginning analysts responded with prompt fervor. The Bitcoin whitepaper made clear that it was in numerous ways subsidiary of prior work, and its objective — a computerized money whose worth could be relied upon without government oversight — was a recognizable objective locally. Today, the whitepaper is held in wonder as the principal guideline for an overall innovation transformation.

Floods of blockchain, digital money, savvy contract, and permissionedledger improvement followed. To comprehend the potential and difficulties of this thriving development, one must initially see the value in Bitcoin and how it became. The blockchain is significantly more than an innovation of money. In any case, that is where it began. What's more, in every way that really matters, a groundbreaking development in finance turns into a change in each and every other area. Cash, the establishment for the measured trade of significant worth, makes the world go around. In the expressions of the history specialist Yuval Noah Harari, "cash is the most general and most effective arrangement of common trust ever created." This is on the grounds that, as the German financial analyst Georg Friedrich Knapp made sense of 100 years back in The State Hypothesis of Cash, what makes money significant isn't the innate worth of an actual resource, like the valuable metals in coins. It is the eagerness of others to acknowledge it. Cash is, at base, a formalization of unadulterated trust. Doubters who guarantee that cryptographic forms of money, for example, bitcoin are essentially worthless in light of the fact that they lay on nothing botch monetary standards for the resources they designate. No significant money in this present reality depends on anything unmistakable. Valid, the US stores a lot of gold in Stronghold Knox. On the off chance that a genuine Auric Goldfinger of James Bond notoriety took everything, notwithstanding, computerized teller machines and supermarket agents wouldn't quit tolerating dollar greenbacks. If a large portion of the world can trust bits of paper and their evenmore- unique computerized portrayals as money, there is no great explanation they can't do likewise for cryptographically characterized cash, for example, bitcoin. All that ultimately matters is whether the applicable money related framework moves the essential certainty. A specific cryptographic money might crash in cost and, surprisingly, go to nothing, however that is not the same as saying digital currency is innately generally worthless by any means. The way that cash addresses a deliberation of significant worth prepared for bitcoin and the blockchain from a subsequent perspective. Current money can take the generally indifferent of resources — a home, say — and change it into outlandish collateralized contract commitments zooming across the screens of overall subordinates dealers with their algorithmic exchanging motors. As such courses of action turn out to be increasingly intricate, the connection between the genuine resources what's more, the monetary instruments turns out to be progressively lessened.

This is the extraordinary commitment of what agents call "securitization." That cycle disentangled in the monetary emergency of 2008. What appeared to the world's most splendid financial backers, investors, and controllers like secure plans crashed practically for the time being. There were unquestionably misuses, and organizations that ought to have been rebuffed all the more seriously for their part in those maltreatments. At last, however, avarice is certainly not an uncommon condition in the monetary area. It the typical situation. Fundamental gamble made the emergency so startling. Instruments that appeared to be broadened and detached, as heaps of thousands of individual home loans, out of nowhere demonstrated exceptionally related. It was not only that a few banks and brokers were conniving — that came as little shock — however that the actual embodiment of current money could presently not be relied upon. The monetary world was not so decentralized as it appeared. Furthermore, in the event that cash couldn't be relied upon, what could? The framework in 2008 was so delicate on the grounds that exchanging movement was decoupled from the genuine resources fundamental those exchanges. Subsidiary monetary instruments, like prospects and choices, have a long history, however both exchanging volumes also, intricacy detonated in ongoing many years. That is to a great extent the outcome of how a previous emergency inside the monetary area was settled. That one made far less titles and appeared to have a flawless goal. However it laid the foundation for the later calamity. Yet again and, the focal subject was trust.

The Buttonwood Understanding of 1792 was a sign of companion topeer (P2P) trust. The stockbrokers gathered under a buttonwood tree not since it had any unique status, but since it was what current game scholars would call a "Schelling point": a sensible spot that any of them would anticipate that the others should pick for a meeting.3 They made a deal to avoid carrying on with work with some other merchants, and to charge each other uniform commissions, since they were not outsiders. They all knew one another and were sure about the attachment of the local area. Any of them could have benefitted, to some degree in the short run, by abandoning from the understanding and exchanging through autonomous barkers. Over the long haul, however, they knew they would be in an ideal situation controlling the provisions of the trade altogether. They confided in their adversaries to adhere to the arrangement since they were additionally their companions what's more, neighbors. The foundation in view of the Buttonwood Understanding — the New York Stock Trade (NYSE) — would develop to turn into the world's generally strong monetary commercial center. These days, it is recorded on to see that an organization the NYSE is adequately proof to regard its authenticity. You needn't bother with to have a ton of familiarity with the part associations of the trade or its administration components to feel sufficiently sure to buy a stock recorded on it. The NYSE today is a strong sign of middle person trust. On its surface, Money Road is one of the most adaptable exchange markets on the planet. The volume of values exchanging has developed to levels that would have been unbelievable years and years prior. Both the trades that interaction exchanges and the exchanging firms that go into them were electronic quite a while in the past, and those PC networks are as often as possible refreshed with more limit and new innovation. However dig further, and the framework looks impressively less high level. At the actual heart of Money Road is the method involved with giving and following portions of corporate stock. The number of offers that has an organization given, and who claims them out of nowhere? Until the 1970s, stock possession was followed through paper authentications. It was what could be compared to P2P trust. Each exchange must be founded on an immediate relationship addressed in the exchange of the endorsement. As exchanging volumes expanded, that construction turned out to be progressively unreasonable. At a certain point, couriers would jumble lower Manhattan with handcarts brimming with stock endorsements, moving them between financier houses to settle a trade.

The exchange could be made in a moment over the telephone or on a modernized framework, yet the real thing of significant worth — the stock declaration — moved similarly that it did in the times of the Buttonwood Understanding. Postponements and mistakes got so awful that the NYSE ground to a virtual stop. The answer for what became known as the "desk work emergency" was to permit business firms to "net" transactions.5 Assuming Morgan Stanley clients purchased 1,000 offers in a day from Merrill Lynch clients, and Merrill Lynch clients purchased 1,000 portions of similar stock from Morgan Stanley clients, there was compelling reason need to send 2,000 divides among the two organizations.

The exchanges essentially offset. Each organization kept its own records of its clients' property, however the framework required a focal store that kept every one of the stock endorsements. This association is the Vault Trust and Clearing Partnership (DTCC), referenced in the prologue to this book. The DTCC furthermore, its auxiliary, Surrender and Company, are actually the record proprietors of basically every portion of stock exchanged the U.S. At the point when financial backers purchase shares, they are really purchasing claims on stock held at the DTCC. There are comparative focal protections safes (CSDs) in other major monetary focuses. The transition to CSDs was a basic move toward the dematerialization of money. The U.S. choice in 1971 to go off the best quality level intended that there was authoritatively nothing backing the buying force of the dollar, other than the full confidence and credit of the public authority. Albeit in pragmatic terms, the dollar had not been an intermediary for valuable metals for quite a while, this step officially settled it as just a token addressing an theoretical worth. The DTCC did likewise for stocks, decoupling the theoretical freedoms of offer possession from the actual launch of authentications. From that point, it was a sluggish however genuinely straight line to the thought t

CHAPTER III

Bitcoin

In this part, we start our examination of Bitcoin. We examine the term, outline the Bitcoin framework from the old style monetary framework, and clarify the outcomes of not having a focal power. We show how the three value-based necessities talked about in segment 1.5.3 are fulfilled and make a reason for the second, more specialized part of this book. After this, we focus on the beginnings, the turn of events, and the political qualities of the Bitcoin framework. The current part fills in as a short rundown furthermore, unpleasant outline that plans to feature the imaginative person of the Bitcoin framework. Bitcoin is an equivocal term. Portraying both the general framework and some is utilized of the subcomponents. The last class incorporates the Bitcoin organization, the Bitcoin (correspondence) convention, and the Bitcoin (money related) unit. The equivocalness of the term creates a great deal of turmoil and presents the primary snag that must be defeated to grasp the framework. We are subsequently going to utilize a severe definitional limit among the different ideas. The term Bitcoin, all alone, will be utilized to allude to the Bitcoin framework or the Bitcoin innovation. At the point when we allude to the subcomponents, we will constantly utilize the terms organization, convention, or unit. Bitcoin is an exhaustive idea that connects a few mechanical parts together so that the units of significant worth are given under contest and have both a virtual portrayal and decentralized exchange handling. Along these lines, the Bitcoin framework has made cash that is significantly not the same as some other cash — like item cash, money, or business bank stores (see figure 2.1). To comprehend the reason why Bitcoin is one of a kind, returning to various types of money is valuable as per their control structures as displayed. There are three aspects. The primary aspect is portrayal. Cash can be addressed in virtual structure or actual structure. The subsequent aspect is exchange dealing with. Cash can be executed in unified or decentralized networks. At last, the third aspect is cash creation. Some monies are made by a syndication while others are given under contest. Cash is addressed by an actual item, typically a coin or bill — implying that its esteem is indistinguishable from the item. The holder of a money unit is consequently the proprietor of the relating esteem. Subsequently, the possession freedoms to the money units, circling uninhibitedly in the economy, are in every case obviously characterized without anybody having to keep records. This element takes into consideration a decentralized installment framework where money can change hands between two specialists without the inclusion of an outsider. In most nations, the national bank or the depository is the syndication backer of money. Product cash, like gold, is likewise addressed by an actual item, and once more, the ongoing holder of a unit is naturally doled out responsibility for esteem unit. Therefore, no record-keeping is expected to involve it as an installment instrument, prompting decentralized exchange handling naturally. Gold varies from cash by its serious creation process since anybody can enter the matter of extricating gold and along these lines make new gold units.

Business bank stores is virtual cash. It exists just as a record in a bookkeeping framework. At the point when an installment is made, the records are changed by deducting the installment sum from the purchaser and attributing it to the dealer. There are numerous ways of starting installments; the most well-known are charge cards, checks, and web based banking. Business banks seek stores; for that reason we think about the making of cash as business bank stores as serious. The banks are liable for keeping records, thus any exchange between a purchaser and a dealer requires a business bank or a few business banks to refresh the particular accounts. Therefore, business bank stores are executed in a unified installment framework. National bank electronicmoney is likewise virtual cash. In many nations, free to electronic national bank cash is confined to monetary mediators. They utilize the assets in these records for settlement purposes and to satisfy hold prerequisites. In difference to business bank stores, national bank stores can be made exclusively by the national bank. exhibits that Bitcoin's key development is the decentralized the executives of responsibility for virtual resource. The extraordinary element of Bitcoin is that it consolidates the value-based benefits of a virtual financial unit with the foundational autonomy of decentralized exchange handling. As we will see all through the book, this development can possibly disturb the ongoing monetary framework also, numerous different areas. To accomplish the remarkable blend of controls portrayed in, Bitcoin utilizes a few parts showed. Bitcoin unit. Bitcoin units are the virtual financial units of the framework. Really they don't exist in actual structure. Bitcoin units are simply record sections that are relegated to a explicit individual.1 Bitcoin organization. The Bitcoin network is completely decentralized. It includes members furthermore, their associations and fills in as an essential channel of correspondence for trading data and building agreement. Bitcoin convention. The Bitcoin convention specifies the available resources by which correspondence inside the Bitcoin network should happen. It fundamentally contains normalized rules on how messages, all things considered, ought to be arranged. Unbalanced cryptography. Unbalanced cryptography (additionally open key cryptography) is utilized for confirmation purposes. It empowers all clients of the Bitcoin organization to decisively confirm the authenticity of any exchange message. Bitcoin blockchain. The Bitcoin blockchain is a public record. Each individual can investigate the record, download a duplicate, and change it. In any case, the organization will as it were think about the variant of the record that contains just exchanges that are irrefutably genuine and is viewed as the latest rendition of the Bitcoin blockchain. The last basis is ensured by an agreement convention. For this, the Bitcoin blockchain uses a technique known as verification of work. The utilization of a record isn't a curiosity credited to Bitcoin innovation. Business bank stores are, for instance, nothing other than a record based virtualization of cases to actual money related units (cash). Here, the record is overseen solely by a focal power that ensures conditional limit, value-based authenticity, and conditional agreement.

Conditional limit connects with tying down the proprietor's ability to start an installment. In an old style banking framework, clients can converse with their client guide or present their installment directions through the bank's internet banking stage. The foundation given by the business bank and other focal specialist organizations guarantees that the exchange will be executed. Without a focal power, executing an installment request in this conventional way is beyond the realm of possibilities. In the Bitcoin framework another chance must accordingly exist that permits members to start exchanges. Value-based authenticity is checked when the exchanges are started. In an old style banking framework, the focal power distinguishes the initiator of the exchange and guarantees that this individual legitimately owns the referred to adjust. The distinguishing proof is typically accomplished by inspecting identifications, written by hand marks, and pin codes or by utilizing biometric distinguishing proof strategies. This large number of control instruments depend on a focal position to deal with the entrance rules. Without even a trace of a focal power with respect to the Bitcoin framework, value-based authenticity must be executed by other implies. In the event that a solitary substance is solely approved to deal with all installment records, as it were one record exists which guarantees conditional agreement of course. Without a trace of a focal authority with respect to the Bitcoin framework, then, at that point, unique, possibly similarly authentic adaptations of the record will exist. For this situation, some other strategy should be utilized to accomplish conditional agreement by figuring out which adaptation of the record addresses the genuine state. The critical development of Bitcoin is its refusal to draw in a focal power. Without a focal power, it is more hard to ensure value-based limit, lay out value-based authenticity, and accomplish conditional agreement. How these necessities are met in the Bitcoin network is portrayed in the accompanying segment.

The Bitcoin network is the underpinning of the framework. It takes into consideration the trading of data
what's more, depends on shared innovation. The term distributed implies that all the network members are equivalent, no matter what, and that correspondence can take place between any two members. There is no focal construction, and no member has any selective honors. Exchanges and different messages are sent inside the Bitcoin organization to lay out agreement. For example, in the event that Edith wishes to send Daniel a Bitcoin unit, she makes a exchange message that contains the separate installment request. The message should be created by the norms of the Bitcoin convention and shipped off somewhere around one of the other organization member. In our model, the exchange message arrives at Tony, who keeps a duplicate of the message and transfers it to his immediate associations; to be specific, Marcia and Michèle. Marcia andMichèle do likewise. The message gets sent until all organization members have gotten a duplicate of it. Albeit the installment request is agreeable to Daniel, the exchange message does not need to be sent straightforwardly to Daniel. Whether and when Daniel learns of this message is at first insignificant. As we will see later, Daniel doesn't need to have a place with Presently the (prompt) gathering of organization members. It is just vital that the exchange is recognized by a greater part of the organization members. The decentralized and dynamic geography of the Bitcoin network is the justification for the framework's remarkable power. On the off chance that singular members disengage from the organization, this can be made up for without an issue, and the correspondence can be proceeded through elective channels. On the off chance that somebody wishes to start an

exchange, it is adequate to transfer the exchange message to any organize member and pause for it to spread by forward. This guideline ensures that the necessity of value-based limit is fulfilled consistently. Correspondence inside the Bitcoin network capabilities with next to no dependence on trust. There are no limitations on affirmation, and members can make quite a few nom de plumes, it difficult to prohibit individual members from the framework. Subsequently, members need to accept that each message they get has been deceitfully modified by the shipper and must thusly be decisively checked for its truth content.

what's more, attempts to decode it utilizing the comparing public key. In the event that Tony can do as such, he then, at that point, realizes that the message was recently encoded utilizing Edith's confidential key. An underlying check of the exchange isn't adequate. Review that the exchange message is handed-off and sent through an untrusted network. Each beneficiary has to check it. On the off chance that Tony advances the exchange message to Marcia and Michèle, both beneficiaries should autonomously confirm that the exchange message is genuine. Specifically, they need to check whether it was truly started by Edith and whether none of the exchange boundaries have been changed. Assuming this subsequent confirmation step would not occur, then, at that point, Tony could change the message (see figure 2.5) and hand-off the adjusted exchange message for Edith. To forestall such a control, Marcia and Michèle will just acknowledge the first scrambled message. They will then, at that point, utilize Edith's public key to confirm the message's realness. Tony, who isn't in control of Edith's confidential key, can't change furthermore, re-scramble the exchange message. Marcia and Michèle have subsequently no trouble distinguishing any deceitful way of behaving. An illustration of a control endeavor is shown in figure 2.5. Michèle and Marcia neglect to decode the message and can subsequently quickly reject the controlled exchange message.

In the event that an exchange message is real, it is designated to the organization members' assortments of checked exchanges. That is fundamentally a line for confirmed messages pausing to be placed into the Bitcoin blockchain. Assuming an organization member gets an exchange message, he needs to guarantee that the exchange was started by the legitimate owner of the particular Bitcoin units. For this reason, Bitcoin utilizes demonstrated cryptographic techniques. Similar cryptographic standards are utilized for internet business, web based banking, and numerous different applications. Responsibility for units requires the elite ownership of a confidential key that is used to cryptographically scramble exchange messages before they are handed-off to the network. For every confidential key, there is a comparing public key. This public key can be used to unscramble any message that has recently been scrambled with the relating confidential key. Rather than the confidential key, the public key is public. Any individual who gets a exchange message can accordingly decode it. The terms encryption and unscrambling are to some degree misdirecting in this specific circumstance. Clearly, the cycle isn't intended to conceal any data. All things considered, everybody is in control of the public key and can in this way decode the exchange message. It is somewhat used to check the beginning and the authenticity of the exchange message. The exchange message must be effectively unscrambled with the public key if it was at first scrambled utilizing the relating private key. Since just the legitimate proprietor is in control of the relating private key, this fills in as verification of the exchange's authenticity. In the event that, for instance, somebody prevails with regards to decoding an exchange message utilizing Edith's public key, this fills in as obvious evidence that the messages has been encoded with Edith's confidential key. Since Edith is the main individual who knows her private key, this technique permits anybody tomathematically confirm that the exchange message was really created by her delineates the strategy utilizing a model. Edith scrambles the exchange message with her confidential key prior to sending it to Tony. Tony gets the message and attempts to decode it utilizing the relating public key. In the event that Tony can do as such, he then, at that point, realizes that the message was recently encoded utilizing Edith's confidential key. An underlying confirmation of the exchange isn't adequate. Review that the exchange message is handed-off and sent through an untrusted network. Each beneficiary has to check it. In the event that Tony advances the exchange message to Marcia and Michèle, both beneficiaries should freely confirm that the exchange message is genuine. Specifically, they need to check whether it was truly started by Edith and whether none of the exchange boundaries have been changed. Assuming that this subsequent confirmation step would not occur, then Tony could change the message and transfer the adjusted exchange message for Edith. To forestall such a control, Marcia and Michèle will just acknowledge the first scrambled message. They will then utilize Edith's public key to check the message's validness. Tony, who isn't in control of Edith's confidential key, can't modify also, re-scramble the exchange message. Marcia and Michèle have accordingly no trouble recognizing any fake way of behaving. An illustration of a control endeavor is represented. Michèle and Marcia neglect to decode the message and can thusly promptly reject the controlled exchange message.

In the event that an exchange message is genuine, it is dispensed to the organization members' assortments

of confirmed exchanges. That is essentially a line for confirmed messages pausing to be placed into the Bitcoin blockchain.Owing to the decentralized idea of the organization, there will definitely be circumstances in which the different exchange lines of the organization members are noticeably off or may try and contain problematic exchanges. Allow us to expect, for instance, that an individual all the while issues and transfers two exchanges, attempting to move similar Bitcoin units to various organization members. In a unified framework, when a contention like this emerges, the exchange that is held to be substantial is the one that arrives at the focal power first. The Bitcoin framework, be that as it may, expressly won't utilize a focal power. As a result, there is no clear pioneer, and it is conceivable that one piece of the organization initially finds out about the first exchange while the remainder of the organization initially finds out about the subsequent exchange. Both exchanges are genuine on the grounds that they have both been given by the legitimate owner of the comparing Bitcoin units. In any case, on the grounds that the two exchanges connect with something similar Bitcoin balance, only one of the them can be legitimate. It Shows a substantial illustration of such a circumstance. Edith all the while sends messages to Tony and Jake. In her message to Tony, she expresses that she wishes to move a particular Bitcoin unit to Daniel. In her message to Jake, she alludes to a similar Bitcoin unit yet replaces the recipient (Daniel) with Lucas. The two messages have been scrambled utilizing Edith's confidential key and are consequently genuine. The messages are transferred and stay in the particular exchange lines of the two gatherings. As of now, Tony, Marcia, andMichèle feel that Edith wishes to move the Bitcoin unit to Daniel while Brian, Jake, and Claudia accept that she needs to send it to Lucas. For the organization overall, it is immaterial which of the two contending exchanges wins. Notwithstanding, to forestall twofold spending and to accomplish agreement among all network members, only one of the two exchanges should be allowed to enter the agreement adaptation of the Bitcoin blockchain. Bitcoin Mining To figure out the agreement component of the

Bitcoin framework, we first need to examine the job of a Bitcoin excavator. A Bitcoin digger gathers forthcoming Bitcoin exchanges, confirms their authenticity, and collects them into what is known as a block.

A block is an information structure that incorporates something like one exchange. The course of collecting blocks and playing out the vital calculations is called Bitcoin mining. An's excavator will likely procure recently made Bitcoin units through this action as made sense of beneath. Bitcoin mining is permissionless however requires computational assets. Each organization member is allowed to conclude how much cash the individual in question wishes to spend on computational assets. To turn into a Bitcoin excavator, an organization client needs the most late duplicate of the Bitcoin blockchain and a product bundle that robotizes the process. To gather a block, a Bitcoin digger chooses exchanges that are holding up in his line (mempool). For a block to be for the most part acknowledged, it should satisfy a particular arrangement of predefined rules. For instance, the included exchanges should be authentic and can't be in struggle with some other exchanges in the ongoing block or in any of the past blocks of the Bitcoin blockchain. In the event that an excavator disregards any of these circumstances, his block will be dismissed by the remainder of the organization. Another significant rule is the purported distinguishing proof number of a block. The distinguishing proof number is acquired by processing the block header's hash esteem utilizing the SHA256d hash capability. We will make sense of the specialized subtleties to some degree II of the book. Here, we need to underscore that the recognizable proof number is significant for two reasons. To start with, any new block should reference the ID number of a past block, consequently producing a sequential chain of blocks or a blockchain. Presents the construction of such a chain. Second, the distinguishing proof number is a significant model for the acknowledgment of a block into the Bitcoin blockchain as made sense of underneath.

Unchanging nature of the Blockchain The ID number is unique3 and is reliant on the items in the block header. Any change of a block header's items will unavoidably cause the recognizable proof number to change. This will present irregularities into the chain structure with the goal that all resulting blocks should be reproduced. On the off chance that somebody changes, for example, an exchange in block 1 of, the recognizable proof number of this block will change. Since the distinguishing proof number of block 1 is referred to in obstruct 2, this reference will likewise must be changed. This change relates to an adjustment of block 2 and will cause its distinguishing proof number to change, which, on the other hand, prompts the need to reassemble block 3, etc. A digger gets the distinguishing proof number by registering the block header's hash esteem utilizing the SHA256d hash capability. For instance, consider the hash an incentive for the text, "This block incorporates exchanges 1, 2, and 3." The ID number of this text, which was determined utilizing the hash capability SHA256d, is

80ac1f5e36cefbdde5d58dbe7379e8532335583b79ab805737e7b4de0bf78ffc.

Presently notice the little change in the first message to "This block incorporates exchanges 1, 2, and 4." It will cause an erratic difference in the distinguishing proof number, which should be visible from the comparing new hash esteem:

3b72098d7f49bf8912010cb87afe0a64d824803d2bf6490cf95b7a198c6dc146
Inferable from the exceptional

attributes of the hash capability that is utilized to create ID numbers, it is difficult to think about what sources of info lead to an ideal objective esteem. This trademark is utilized in the mining system as follows. For a block possibility to be acknowledged by all organization members, its distinguishing proof number unquestionable requirement have a very uncommon component: The number should be under a specific limit esteem, that is, it should show a few zeroes toward the start of the recognizable proof number. An illustration of an ID number of a block that was added to the Bitcoin blockchain in 2010 is given in the accompanying model:

000000000a93f114165c1c6940dc5a55ea20a5651af1e9ef0415319ad7458fc9.

Since it is difficult to think about what data sources lead to an ideal recognizable proof number, the main choice the Bitcoin excavators have is to evaluate different block contents until they experience, by unadulterated possibility, an information blend that yields an adequately little distinguishing proof number. For this reason, a block incorporates an information field (called the nonce) that contains inconsistent data.Minersmodify this erratic information to acquire new ID numbers. These changes don't influence the arrangement of included exchanges. On the off chance that aminer prevails with regards to making a block up-and-comer with an ID number beneath the ongoing edge worth, the individual transmissions the block competitor as fast as conceivable to the organization. The wide range of various organization members can then effectively confirm that the recognizable proof number fulfills the limit rule by registering it themselves. Agreement The agreement amongminers is that each digger who gets a block that incorporates just substantial exchanges and has an ID number that is underneath the current edge adds this block to their own duplicate of the Bitcoin blockchain. From a game hypothetical viewpoint, a technique profile where all excavators add legitimate blocks to their own duplicates of the Bitcoin blockchain is a Nash balance. On the off chance that an excavator accepts that any remaining diggers are acting as needs be, then the best reaction for that excavator is to add a substantial block contender to their own duplicate of the Bitcoin blockchain. A deviation isn't beneficial in light of the fact that it isn't productive to chip away at a variant of the Bitcoin blockchain that isn't by and large acknowledged. Any prize for tracking down blocks on a variant of the chain that isn't acknowledged by any other individual is useless. In this way, in spite of the fact that there is no authority upholding this standard and excavators are allowed to adjust their duplicate of the Bitcoin blockchain as they wish, there is serious areas of strength for a to observe this guideline. This self-implementing rule permits the organization to keep up with agreement about the responsibility for all Bitcoin units. Mining is costly as the calculations utilize a lot of power and are progressively subject to exceptionally specific equipment.

The agreement component is in this way called "confirmation of work." On the off chance that an excavator finds a substantial ID number for a all things considered, played out countless expensive calculations. Adding bogus data (e.g., ill-conceived exchanges) to a block would ruin the block and basically squander every one of the calculations. Seeing as a legitimate ID number is hence evidence that the digger assisted with keeping up with the Bitcoin framework. A singular block can be determined in parts of a second utilizing a customary PC. From the outset, this speed could be seen as a benefit. Notwithstanding, creating blocks at such a high velocity would make it difficult to accomplish agreement. New blocks would be fundamentally more immediately produced than they could be traded over the Bitcoin organization. To balance this issue, the trouble to track down a substantial ID number limits the creation pace of legitimate blocks misleadingly. The Bitcoin framework adjusts the limit number after each 2,016 blocks (generally every fourteen days) to keep a ten-minute normal per block, free of the generally computational assets utilized in mining. The imbalance in costs between finding an answer and confirming it plays an especially significant job. Finding a legitimate block is incredibly intriguing.

Interestingly, it is not difficult to check that a given block has a legitimate distinguishing proof number. It takes the organization members a negligible part of one moment to do as such. Since all diggers realize that a proposed block will get checked by any remaining members, they just remember authentic exchanges for their blocks. A block containing ill-conceived exchanges wouldn't be acknowledged by the rest of the organization regardless of whether it had a substantial distinguishing proof number. Anybody not playing by the rules would in this manner squander registering assets. By agreement, network members acknowledge the longest chain as the present status of the record. The rationale behind that arrangement is that the longest chain is the one that requires the most noteworthy measure of assets to be registered, making it the one with the broadest help and, much more significant, over the top expensive to change. Specifically, it is simply conceivable to roll out an improvement in the event that a digger had the assets to collect blocks with a higher likelihood than the remainder of the organization. Just an organization member who controls in excess of 50% of the framework's in general computational assets would be in a situation to accomplish this. In the event that an organization member wishes, for instance, to change the third block of the chain in figure 2.8, he should reference the second block in the chain and create an adequate measure of new blocks to have the option to surpass the prevailing agreement variant of the chain. The wide range of various diggers will at the same time create new blocks based on block 6 of the longest chain. The going after network member hence needs to create new blocks more rapidly than the wide range of various organization members. The farther back in the agreement chain a block is found, the more troublesome it will become to change this block. A block's trustworthiness is hence safeguarded by the chain. Yet again assuming we presently go to our model in figure 2.6, it ought to be clear how agreement is accomplished. Jake, Brian, and Claudia will remember the exchange for favor of Lucas into their block applicant. Tony, Marcia, and Michèle will rather incorporate the exchange for Daniel.

Which of the two exchanges wins will rely upon which excavator is quick to create a legitimate block. When a substantial block including one of the two clashing exchanges has been produced effectively, different diggers have a motivation to follow the longest chain and keep on chipping away at this new variant of the blockchain. Realizing that the other exchange would be dismissed, diggers will dispose of the exchange. As displayed in figure 2.9, the chain can foster in a few headings contingent upon which digger creates the following block. Mining Prize Mining is exorbitant. The equipment must be obtained and kept up with, also, there are power costs. These expenses are conveyed independently by the diggers. On the other hand, keeping up with the Bitcoin blockchain helps all organization members. In this regard, mining gives a public decent: nobody can rejected from use the organization, and all organization members benefit from the mining movement. No excavator, in any case, would have an impetus to contribute and to bear the expense of keeping up with the organization on the off chance that there were no remuneration. The Bitcoin framework tackles this motivation issue by permitting excavators to add a socalled coinbase exchange to each impede. This exchange produces new Bitcoin units that can be guaranteed by the excavator who has effectively added the block to the Bitcoin blockchain. Since everybody is following the longest form of the chain, the coinbase exchange might be acknowledged by the organization assuming the block is to be sure important for the longest rendition of the blockchain. In our model, on the off chance that Brian created a legitimate block, this block would contain Edith's exchange to Lucas as well as the coinbase exchange for him. On the off chance that Marcia prevailed with regards to producing a legitimate block, then the exchange would, all things being equal, contain Edith's exchange to Daniel as well as the coinbase exchange for her. The two exchanges contained in Marcia's and Brian's block up-and-comers are represented in figure 2.10. Just like with any remaining exchanges, the coinbase exchange is substantial provided that it is kept in the longest adaptation of the chain. This cycle propels excavators to The Fantasy of Virtual Money The most vital move toward Bitcoin happened in 1982 with David Chaum's development of Digi-Cash. [55] Chaum contended that current electronic installment frameworks would impressively confine individual security and would create detectable installment streams of delicate information. This issue propelled him to foster a virtual financial unit that would mimic the namelessness of money. In spite of the fact that DigiCash depends on monopolistic cash creation and unified exchange handling, the commutativity of the applied cryptographic processes works with a framework in which the national bank aimlessly signs the financial units and in this manner has no data about the chronic quantities of extraordinary financial units. Accordingly, the chronic numbers can't be allocated to people, and the financial units are utilized secretly. Value-based agreement is accomplished through an incorporated record. On the off chance that a money related unit is utilized, then its chronic number should be introduced to the national bank. If the number isn't in the national bank's record, it is accepted that the financial unit is being utilized interestingly and is in this manner legitimate. Assuming that the chronic number is now enlisted by the national bank, it is viewed as an endeavored twofold spend and as needs be obstructed. While this approach unquestionably gives some level of namelessness, it actually has a focal place of assault and isn't restriction safe. The goal to foster a mysterious virtual money related unit was additionally fortified by Timothy C. May's Crypto Revolutionary Manifesto. The declaration was first

introduced at the CRYPTO '88 Meeting yet distributed on paper later. He anticipated a social change that would be driven by the mechanical conceivable outcomes of cryptography that would permit another sort of financial collaboration, which would be free of the potential limitations and responses of a transcendent state. To accomplish this, it would be especially important to have virtual financial units and official agreements that capability in an unknown (or pseudonymous) setting. In 1998, the PC researcher Wei Dai, who was obviously affected by the Crypto Rebel Statement, distributed a short paper introducing the possibility of b-cash, a pseudonymous virtual financial unit. In the b-cash framework, public keys were

utilized as aliases, which credit or charge exchanges could be relegated. Value-based authenticity is ensured by a mark utilizing the comparing private key of the charged person. All (or on the other hand a subgroup) of the members make due separate records that contain the records of the ongoing adjusts of all aliases. The article contains no substantial proposition on the most proficient method to accomplish conditional agreement. All things considered, b-cash is introduced as a psychological test that proposes the presence of a coordinated correspondence channel. The cash creation follows a cutthroat process, utilizing numeric riddles that must be addressed through escalated calculation in any case, that can be checked essentially. The costs caused by the cash creation process are with no obvious end goal not entirely settled by the framework's parameterization.7 The idea of making in any case paltry undertakings falsely costly traces all the way back to the commitments of Adam Backas well as Cynthia Dwork and Moni Naor[85] and was initially created to battle disavowal of-administration (DoS) assaults and spam email. These commitments are the reason for the evidence of-work agreement convention that is utilized in the Bitcoin framework. In 2005, Hal Finney introduced the possibility of the reusable verification of-work system. His move toward consolidated the thoughts ofWei Dai and Adam Back. Afterward, Hal Finney became one

of the main Bitcoin clients and the beneficiary of the primary Bitcoin transaction.It was likewise in 2005 that Scratch Szabo distributed a blog entry on Piece Gold. The article portrays the use of the confirmation of-work calculation for serious cash creation while simultaneously getting a public record. Despite the fact that Szabo's blog entry was not cited in the Bitcoin publication, it very well may be accepted that Piece Gold contributed significantly toward Bitcoin's turn of events. Bitcoin was distributed on October 31, 2008, by a creator, or group of creators, under the nom de plume Nakamoto.8 The publication[158] showed up in the style of an scholastic article on a mailing list for cryptography. It is, nonetheless, still indistinct today whose character or personalities are concealed by the alias. Aside from the writer's character, the article (and the reference execution) reveals complete, definite data about the Bitcoin technology.9 The creator has no honors inside the framework and has become unessential inferable from the revelation of the data as well as its resulting innovative advancement by others. By the by, this ought to in no way, shape or form reduce the accomplishment of the originator. It ought to be noted here that the mysterious creator was designated for a Nobel prize in financial matters by UCLA Teacher Bhagwan Chowdhry Bitcoin has a decentralized construction and is totally open source. There is no concentrated authority, no organization, and no person who has extraordinary honors to decide its future turn of events. Bitcoin is a develop that is rejuvenated by the system activity, everything being equal. Its freedom from any substantial element is an intentional plan decision and a potential clarification for why the innovator wishes to remain mysterious.

Be that as it may, the shortfall of initiative suggests various conversation starters and harbors the peril that the framework could fall into turmoil. Specifically, the two following inquiries emerge.

1. What occurs assuming the innovation is duplicated and somebody makes their own "Bitcoin" units?

2. Who will decide the future advancement of the Bitcoin framework and how could potential issues be taken care of and the innovation be adjusted?

Bitcoin Duplicates: Alleged Altcoins Bitcoin's source code is public. This has the result that each individual can duplicate it, change it in any capacity wanted, and distribute an elective rendition of the framework.

This doesn't mean, nonetheless, that extra Bitcoin units can be made. Bitcoin clones lay out new, obviously separate money related units, which have their own records. Such duplicates are named altcoins. For example, we could make Bookcoin; another digital currency, intensely enlivened by Bitcoin, for the perusers of this book. Bookcoin could address a precise duplicate of the Bitcoin innovation or be defined in an unexpected way. Instances of boundaries that could be changed are the absolute stockpile of coins or the typical opportunity to create a legitimate block. To make a new altcoin, the creatormodifies a duplicate of the Bitcoin source code and recompiles it. Throughout the span of time, a large number of such altcoins have appeared. Some of them have a lengthy scope of capabilities or vary essentially in definition, but many are essentially Bitcoin duplicates that bear another name. Regardless of this opposition, Bitcoin is plainly the pioneer among cryptographic forms of money. It has a first-mover advantage and name acknowledgment. Further, because of organization impacts the market capitalization of Bitcoin money related units is significantly higher than the wide range of various cryptocurrencies. Organization and Development of the Bitcoin Framework The motivation structures inside the Bitcoin framework are set so that every member's very own result is amplified by keeping the ongoing guidelines. Vitalik Buterin makes sense of this peculiarity in the first issue of the BitcoinMagazine. He contends that Bitcoin is the main PC organization where extortion is blocked not in light of exclusive limitations but rather on the grounds that no one can acquire a benefit by digressing singularly from these principles. One unquestionable necessity, in any case, know that Bitcoin includes programming, and that product can be altered. Changes are carried out if an adequately huge piece of organization members settle on the progressions and benefit from the alteration. The decentralized administration of the Bitcoin framework includes a diverse popularity based interaction of the greatest intricacy. A definitive investigation is beyond the realm of possibilities, and an endeavor would surpass the extent of this book. By and by, we might want to examine this point in a short presentation and feature a portion of the framework's generally significant determinants. Before we start our investigation, we might want to pressure the key significance to have a framework that considers some development over the long run. A rigorously static situation could have horrendous outcomes and even lead to framework disappointment. If, for instance, a security break is distinguished that must be fixed assuming the innovation is modifiable,

most clients should seriously mull over this a genuine motivation to change the product. Be that as it may, there might be subtler reasons that make it beneficial to change the Bitcoin framework, for example, a wish to broaden its scope of capabilities, to get long haul soundness, or to incorporate new highlights. Data sources and proposition for such changes are presented through different decentralized channels furthermore, can be put together by anybody. Questions with respect to how these thoughts ought to be carried out are typically discussed openly. Gatherings and mailing records are well known conversation stages utilized for this reason. The Bitcoin Improvement Proposition (BIP) process is by a wide margin the main instrument that is utilized to formalize dynamic thoughts. [209] BIPs should be formed utilizing a compulsory design and should incorporate a legitimization it are important to state why the upgrades. Also, they should give specialized
details.

Assuming that a proposition is so unequivocally challenged that no broad agreement can be reached, it can then, at that point, be decided on. Just excavators can partake in these votes. An excavator submits a vote at whatever point he effectively creates a substantial block.12 A proposition will be acknowledged on the off chance that it accomplishes a recommended rate number of "yes" votes inside a formerly determined stretch (e.g., inside the last 1,000 blocks decides of acknowledgment with the end goal that the new guidelines are a subset of the old principles. Therefore, blocks that are legitimate under the new programming will likewise be acknowledged as substantial under the old programming, however most frequently, not the other way around. A hard fork alludes to a fork where the new programming widens the acknowledgment standards with the end goal that the old principles address a subset of the new guidelines. This has the result that blocks made utilizing the new programming can be dismissed by the old programming. On the other hand, the new programming will continuously consider blocks that are produced with the old programming as substantial. A constrained fork utilizes something else entirely set where the old programming won't ever acknowledge blocks as per the new principles as well as the other way around. It consequently will continuously lead to two separate adaptations of the blockchain.

Assuming that the record is stretched out by a block that has been produced with the old programming, this may for sure briefly make a few renditions of the record be produced; notwithstanding, the predominance of the new programming normally guarantees that the record develops more rapidly, applying the new guidelines. Since this record is likewise legitimate under the old standards, every one of the members will relocate to this form when it turns into the longest adaptation of the blockchain. A hard fork, then again, must be settled through the predominance of the old programming. In the event that the new programming can win, two variants of the record will endure: one as indicated by the old principles and one as per the new principles. Constrained forks are neither forward-nor in reverse viable and can't be

broken down. Programming overhauls are a lot more straightforward to accomplish on the off chance that they can be executed utilizing a delicate fork. With a delicate fork, even nonupdated network assets can be utilized couple with the new programming. With a hard fork, in any case, every asset should be refreshed exclusively. Anybody who is running framework that has not been refreshed will not be able to take part in the organization. Figure 2.13 shows a course of events of probably the most popular Bitcoin forks. In spite of the fact that there have been many forking occasions, the elective record renditions partake in a moderately low ubiquity. Just the diggers are straightforwardly engaged with the recently considered choice cycles as to additional advancement of the Bitcoin framework. Different members in the Bitcoin framework, like shippers, clients, or financial backers, have no immediate impact either by express democratic or by settling forks. One could subsequently contend that the political process is overwhelmed by a select gathering of partners. Specifically, the way that diggers can have their own personal objectives that may not really be in that frame of mind of the entire Bitcoin framework might raise worries about the manageability of the interaction. To some degree, these reactions are legitimate. In any case, it would be misleading to expect to be just the Bitcoin framework is only constrained by diggers. Other client bunches have a number of manners by which they can impact advancement and shape the fate of the Bitcoin framework. To begin with, all members have the chance to present recommendations, to partake in the

political talk, and to impact general assessment. Second, a verifiable type of blackball right exists. In the event that a change is executed against the desire of different gatherings of partners, deliberate vulnerabilities and dangers can create. This will then, at that point, have negative repercussions on the acknowledgment and the market cost of the Bitcoin unit, which is equivalent to a fall in the diggers' truly monetary reward. An illustration of a change that fizzled regardless of the help of in excess of 80% among diggers is SegWit2x. The constrained fork was proclaimed dropped in a joint explanation by the six initiators because of fears of partitioning the local area. [23] Third, many changes require a hard fork. As examined over, a hard fork requires that every asset must be refreshed independently with the new programming. Really at that time will traders, clients, network hubs, and any remaining assets support the changed variant of the agreement convention and consider exchanges and blocks in light of it to be legitimate. [7] Along these lines, even with comprehensively based endorsement, it is incredibly hard to carry out a hard fork. Specifically, on the off chance that a hard fork is constrained against the desire of the nonmining network members, the diggers are in danger of running an elective record without any clients or foundation. The past conversation is in no way, shape or form definitive. Rather, it is expected to feature

the intricacy of navigation and to show that altogether more partners are engaged with this interaction than a shallow assessment proposes. Specifically, diggers can't drive the framework to develop against the desire of the remainder of the organization. This intricacy prompts generally couple of changes and an exceptionally hearty base layer. 2009 The primary Bitcoin exchanges were completed only for testing. The Bitcoin units were minimal more than electronic play cash with no genuine monetary worth and were frequently moved for nothing to new clients. Over the span of the year, the client base developed and with it the quantity of exchanges. In mid-2009, roughly 200 exchanges each day were recorded, and albeit the Bitcoin unit has no key worth a cost increment was accomplished on account of its set number and the interest for the fundamental technology. A first cost gauge was made on October 5, 2009. In light of the then typical power costs for the creation cycle, the cost of a Bitcoin unit was approximated to be US\$0.000764.[160]

2010 On February 6, 2010, Bitcoin Market was the main stage to permit Bitcoin units to be traded for neighborhood cash. The firstmarket exchanges were completed onMarch 17, 2010. The assistance, along with gatherings and a web transfer visit (IRC) channel, was instrumental in deciding the market cost. The main recorded acquisition of merchandise with Bitcoin units traces all the way back to May 22, 2010. The bitcointalk client laszlo concurred in an online forum to pay 10,000 Bitcoin units for two pizzas.15 An immediate buy was unrealistic as of now on the grounds that the conveyance administration would have rather not acknowledged any Bitcoin units. Four days after the solicitation to delicate, laszlo had the option to find a counterparty. The client jercos paid roughly US$25 for the pizzas, utilizing his Mastercard and getting the Bitcoin units consequently. The laszlo pizzas have now acquired faction status and are a significant reference point in Bitcoin's cost history. This exchange denoted a notable conversion scale of US$0.0025 (or on the other hand one fourth of one penny) per one Bitcoin unit and established the groundwork for additional ware buys utilizing this cryptocurrency.16 In July 2010, costs rose to US$0.08 per Bitcoin unit. Simultaneously, the scandalous Japanese Bitcoin trade market MtGox started operating.[157] MtGox was initially arranged as an exchanging stage for an (on the web) dream card game,17 however it was changed over into a site for exchanging Bitcoin units July 2010.18 [163] The stage soon had a generally high volume and empowered a pretty much delegate market cost arrangement. Once more, the cost at last rose and arrived at the US$0.5 level for a brief time frame on November 7 yet before long fell back to values somewhere in the range of US$0.2 and 0.3. 2011 This was trailed by a further sharp cost increment so the US$ equality was penetrated interestingly on February 10, 2011. The rise in cost was covered with the send off of the darknet stage Silk Street, which probably had a huge effect on the early value advancement of the Bitcoin unit. The site was sent off in February 2011 and permitted mysterious exchanging of labor and products. Silk Street advanced into a flourishing business sector for a wide range of unlawful substances and questionable administrations where Bitcoin was utilized as the selective strategy for payment. June 10, 2011, the Bitcoin unit arrived at another pinnacle of just shy of US$32. The cost increment reached a brief conclusion with the hacking of the MtGox stage in that same month. The assailants prevailed with regards to assuming control over client accounts on MtGox and made deals orders with intentionally low costs. This had a huge adverse consequence on certainty and was logical one of the game changers at the cost droop in the following months. This cost improvement later became known as The Incomparable Air pocket of 2011.

Simultaneously, Wikileaks sent off a Bitcoin gift choice that permitted similar individuals to help the stage with Bitcoin units. This occasion had a very significant effect on Bitcoin's cost improvement in that it showed a definitive benefit of utilizing Bitcoin units. Toward the finish of 2010, the web-based installment administration Paypal ended its business relationship with Wikileaks and in this manner truly hampered their raising support crusade. Bitcoin exchanges can't be obstructed. This opened up an free kind of revenue for Wikileaks while it permitted Wikileaks' allies to dispense their gifts as wanted. 2012 On May 9, a report by the Government Department of Examination (FBI) [93] was distributed bringing up the risks of Bitcoin. Simultaneously it expressed that Bitcoin units are simply one more choice for crooks and that one shouldn't anticipate that Bitcoin should supplant existing choices to fund criminal operations. The report additionally made sense of that Bitcoin exchanges are not mysterious and by and large would permit the crooks to be recognized. The report caused a significant media reaction. Over the year, the quantity of acknowledgment focuses for Bitcoin units expanded fundamentally. Bitpay, an enormous installment specialist co-op, declared on September 11, 2012, that it began working with in excess of 1,000 organizations around the world, including numerous cafés as well as various strange organizations like dental specialists and burial service homes. On November 15, WordPress, a huge and globally dynamic organization, followed with its blog facilitating administration. On November 28, a significant achievement was accomplished: Block 210,000 was made, furthermore, interestingly a prize of 25 Bitcoins was paid out rather than the typical 50 Bitcoin units. The purported Block Prize Dividing Day denoted the start of a time of rising costs, and a few voices are heard saying that this occasion was the reason for the abrupt cost increment. According to a monetary perspective, notwithstanding, this speculation is sketchy as it was predictable that the development rate would be divided and that the assumption ought to have been evaluated in as of now. 2013 The year 2013 was one in which Bitcoin pulled in a lot of media consideration due to its outrageous cost instability. The market cost of the Bitcoin unit rose consistently toward the start of the year and got through the past high of US$35 around the start of Spring. In mid-Walk, a product blunder finishing in an impermanent fork in the register prompted a present moment (intraday) value fall of in excess of 20% (see box 2.5). Nonetheless, the negative cost impacts were brief. The political circumstance in Cyprus19 filled the interest for elective speculations past government reach, furthermore, the cost crested over the US$200 blemish on April 9. At the point when the circumstance in Cyprus quieted down once more, the Bitcoin cost dropped altogether. Toward the start of May, reports arose that the first completely practical Bitcoin Mechanized TellerMachine (ATM) had been introduced in San Diego. As indicated by a report from NEWS10 ABC, the machine permitted the buy and offer of the cryptographic money against US$.[1] As it happened in no time a while later, the ATM was just introduced at a press conference.[204] The first openly available fixed Bitcoin ATM became functional in Vancouver on October 28, 2013. The presentation was incredibly effective; on the first day a turnover was accomplished adding up to a five-digit aggregate in (Canadian) dollars.

On October 2, Silk Street was closed somewhere near the FBI and Ross Ulbricht, the supposed site head, was captured in a public library in San Francisco.[185] From that point forward, rebirths of the site have showed up every once in a while. The Bitcoin cost recorded a momentary downfall of around 20% yet recuperated in something like one day and started to rise once more. Barely a month after the fact, the U.S. Senate held a consultation named "Past Silk Street: Expected Dangers, Dangers, and Commitments of Virtual Currencies."[65,66] Different specialists were welcomed, and the dangers and capability of virtual money units were examined. In the days following the meeting, the Bitcoin cost rose decisively and arrived at US$1,216.39 on November 29.20 The for the most part sure course of the conference and the most important moves toward lawful sureness are by and large viewed as the primary purposes behind this increment. A second explanation that is in many cases seen as the reason for the gigantic cost rise is the high request from Chinese financial backers. This hypothesis is upheld specifically by the planning of the resulting cost droop, which was joined by administrative intercession by the Chinese National Bank on December 5. Confidential people were dependent upon more prominent obstacles, trades were dependent upon stricter administrative systems, and monetary delegates were precluded from exchanging Bitcoin units. [181] A few examiners expect that neither the expanded lawful sureness coming about because of the conclusion of Silk Street and the meeting nor the popularity from China were dependable at the record costs. There are signs that the cost was driven primarily by false control on the biggest exchanging stage MtGox.[203] Notwithstanding a huge year-end decline, the Bitcoin cost in 2013 shut at around 5,400 percent of the cost toward the start of the year. 2014 On January 9, 2014, the internet based retailer Overload declared that it would from this time forward acknowledge Bitcoin units as method for payment,[169] making it the main in a number of huge organizations. This was trailed by declarations from the satellite television administrator Dish[80] (May), the web-based travel service Expedia[63]

(June), and Dell[62] (July) as well as Time Inc. [215] andMicrosoft [155] (both December, with Microsoft pulling out its acknowledgment toward the start of 2016).[156] Meanwhile, there have been an ever increasing number of reports of issues with Bitcoin withdrawals on the MtGox exchanging platform.[92] Toward the start of February, a general stop on withdrawals was imposed.21 The action was legitimate by the purported exchange pliability, an issue that can prompt challenges of distinguishing exchanges. When MtGox at long last went disconnected fourteen days after the fact and needed to petition for financial protection, many individuals lost an enormous piece of their Bitcoin units. All things considered, Bitcoin units worth a portion of a billion US$ have vanished on the MtGox trade. Before long, various signs seemed demonstrating that the robbery of the Bitcoin units didn't have anything to do with the claimed cause.[77,203] Notwithstanding the immediate loss of around 850,000 Bitcoin units shared with the stage, the occasions had extensive adverse consequences on the standing of the whole Bitcoin framework, which couldn't be held back in spite of a joint public statement of the leftover enormous Bitcoin companies.[86] For some individuals Bitcoin was MtGox. The Bitcoin unit lost roughly 60% of its worth in 2014. 2015 On January 4, the terrible news with respect to unified trade stages proceeded. The Bitstamp stage was hacked and Bitcoin units worth about US$5.1 million were taken. This was trailed by a further 10 percent drop in costs to US$270, which gone on after a concise time of recuperation, so the Bitcoin unit was briefly exchanging beneath the US$200 mark in mid-January. After a powerless beginning to the year, the Bitcoin unit changed somewhere in the range of US$200 and US$300 for a significant part of the initial 3/4 of the year. The year was likewise portrayed by high funding speculations. The Bitcoin organization 21 Inc, which got risk capital of around US$116 million in Spring, merits an exceptional notice. Among January and October 2015 alone, the openly uncovered funding interests in Bitcoin and blockchain organizations added up to simply under a portion of a billion US$.[64] Then again, the last form of the New York BitLicense Regulation[161] from the start of June was almost certain to inhibitorily affect further ventures as well as on the market cost of the Bitcoin unit. In October, a sharp ascent in costs at long last set in, raising the market cost of the Bitcoin unit to over US$400. In addition to other things, the increment is probably going to have been driven by more tight capital controls in China[180] and the October 22 choice by the European Court of Equity [41] on exception from the worth added charge (Tank). [173] Likewise, the expanded media presence because of new reports about the character of Satoshi Nakamoto could at least be incompletely liable for the rise (see box 2.2).

The Bitcoin unit shut 2015 with a cost of US$430. 2016 The year started with a little downturn in Bitcoin costs, which was supplanted by a delayed vertical pattern. In Spring and April, a progression of hacks from the ShapeShift.io trade stage pulled in media consideration. The help was disrupted by an representative and afterward ransacked a few times. Altogether, nearly US$200,000 was taken in various cryptographic forms of money. Client resources were not impacted due to ShapeShift.io's business model.[222] Bitcoin's cost advancement remained moderately stable during these occasions, and the delayed vertical pattern proceeded. Toward the finish of May, the pattern finished in a hazardous increment of around 70%. This was trailed by a rectification until the cost at last settled between US$600 also, 700 in mid-June. Potential triggers of the huge cost increment are market vulnerabilities because of an English EU mandate (Brexit), as well as the Bitcoin Prize Splitting Occasion toward the start of July. On June 18, without further ado before the Brexit choice, Bitcoin accomplished the greatest cost of US$780 in over two years. Toward the start of August, Bitfinex, a significant Hong Kong based trade, was effectively gone after, and Bitcoin units adding up to US$60 million were taken. When the burglary became known, the Bitcoin cost was at that point in decline. It tends to be expected that the insight about the hack adversely affects the cost and has smothered any opportunity of potential revisions. The cost fell altogether underneath US$600 at times. At the point when the main significant frenzy had passed and obviously the bankruptcy of Bitfinex could be deflected, a consistent vertical pattern started. The ascent in costs might have been filled by the vulnerabilities encompassing the American official political decision and expanded movement in China. 2017 Of every 2017, Bitcoin has been driven into the worldwide spotlight to a degree already incomprehensible. The cost expanded pointedly and numerous other blockchain exercises started to frame. Everybody was abruptly discussing blockchain and digital forms of money. Toward the start of the year, Bitcoin's cost was around US$1,000. Toward the finish of the year on December 17, the Bitcoin unit exchanged at US$19,500. While Bitcoin stayed the prevailing cryptoasset consistently, Ethereum, the second biggest public blockchain, seemingly contributedmore to the frenzy in 2017. Ethereum is a permissionless brilliant agreement stage that is fairly more adaptable than Bitcoin. In specific, it permits anybody to effortlessly make purported tokens — that is, new cryptoassets that can be exchanged on the Ethereum blockchain (see area 7.2). While elective ways to deal with make tokens on the Bitcoin base layer (shaded coins) or through extra layers (Mastercoin/Omni) have existed for some time, in 2017 symbolic issuance and taking care of turned out to be a lot simpler thanks to shrewd agreement based tokens.[188] specifically, a savvy contract standard, typically alluded to as ERC-20, can be utilized to make these tokens in practically no time. Business visionaries — and sadly too numerous con artists — began to issue and sell tokens through purported introductory coin contributions (ICOs), promising that they could be utilized for a future utility or qualifies the proprietor for an installment stream — that is, a profit or an interest installment. These tokens became exceptionally famous, with numerous financial backers being uninformed about the dangers. Specifically, since these tokens incorporate commitments, they are liable to counterparty risk. The rapture lead to dark episodes. Indeed, even undertakings with no current item or client base and groups with almost no related knowledge had the option to raise a great many dollars. The high movement with these symbolic potential customer to an expanded interest for Bitcoin and Ether.22 By and large, individuals initially needed to purchase Bitcoin or Ether to have the option to take part in the symbolic deals. Besides, when somebody needed to sell a token on a trade, this individual typically sold the tokens for Bitcoin or Ether. The worth of Ether became over 13,000 percent in 2017. Thusly, the presence of Bitcoin andmore by and large cryptoassets were progressively seen by monetary establishments like business banks, national banks, and monetary controllers. The way that the fantastic expansion in cost was trailed by a cost crash in 2018 just sped up the conversation. At this point, one can securely say that most people and organizations have an assessment on Bitcoin. "Bitcoin" has likely become one of the most amazing known "brands" today.

The exchange expenses expanded all through 2017 and topped in high twofold digit dollar sums toward the year's end. One clarification absolutely is the more appeal for Bitcoin exchanges. High charges are basically a consequence of the expense market in real life. The increment filled the scaling banter that ruled a large part of the year (see segment 6.2). The main proposition were isolated observer (SegWit) to set up the organization for secondlayer scaling and different types of block size increments. Moreover there has been a recommendation that attempted to arrive at agreement among the local area by joining SegWit with a block size increment. This proposition has been called SegWit2x — SegWit initiation furthermore a block size increment. On July 21, SegWit has effectively been enacted by means of a delicate fork. This occurred

after much discussion and an extensive stretch of vulnerability. Presently, on August 1, a minority of the local area chose to expand the block size (close by some other changes) and accordingly made the Bitcoin Money or B-Money constrained fork. The SegWit2x proposition had been removed as of November 2017 (see area 2.5.3). 2018 The year 2018 was the time of retribution. One of the most lovely cost bubbles throughout the entire existence of cash burst. Bitcoin's cost arrived at a low of around US$3,200 on December 15, 2018. The costs of most ICO tokens and other cryptoassets were butchered considerably more emphatically. The normal low for these resources was around 90 to 95% underneath the unequaled high. This cost droop additionally impacted the public discussion.Many savants arose, guaranteeing that Bitcoin and the entire space of cryptoassets have no future. For instance, inOctober 2018 Nouriel Roubini expressed that "Bitcoin is the 'mother of all tricks' and blockchain is most advertised tech ever." [61] The CEO (President) of JPMorgan, Jamie Dimon, is likewise popular for slamming Bitcoin.[236] He is known for having said that "Bitcoin is a extortion" and will ultimately "explode" and that "any merchant exchanging bitcoin" will be "terminated for being idiotic." It didn't help the standing of the crypto space that many ICOs were out and out tricks. Powerless groups, feeble thoughts, and frail executions of thoughts were wild. Further, the income sans work that could be acquired through an ICO pulled in numerous back-stabbers. Bitcoin's scaling banter turned out to be much more savage in 2018, and frightful infights started to arise. The public allegations and dangers between the various camps wiped out any certainty that was left after the lofty value decline of the main quarter. Nonetheless, in the background there have been numerous extremely sure advancements on the specialized front in 2018. The Lightning Organization has been tried on mainnet, and in excess of 2,000 hubs have been made over 2018.23 The Lightning Organization is one of a few scaling recommendations that takes into consideration a practically limitless number of Bitcoin exchanges at immaterial expenses and without troubling the Bitcoin blockchain (see area 6.2). Other than the Lightning Organization there have been different enhancements. Specifically, the overall framework worked around Bitcoin and other cryptoassets has turn out to be more expert. 2019 began generally calm, at a sticker cost of US$3,800, with littlemedia consideration. It was only after Q2 that the value started to get and before long crossed the US$10,000 mark prior to withdrawing again to about US$7,000 before the year's over.

All through 2019, news arose of blockchain projects by laid out organizations. In June, for instance, Facebook declared Libra, a blockchain-based stablecoin (see box 6.2). While the Libra project proposition was intensely concentrated and apparently had minimal in a similar manner as the Bitcoin blockchain, it took the point back to the spotlight. Additionally, the proposition pressed customary players, specifically national banks, to give their own retail National Bank Computerized Monetary forms (CDBC). The Individuals' Bank of China (PBOC) was one of numerous national banks freely expressing that they would investigate blockchain innovation and present a CBDC. In segment 6.1.5, we contend that these advanced monetary forms won't be permissionless nor decentralized and subsequently sabotage the principal selling recommendation of public blockchains. As of the finish of 2019, a few wallets and DAPP programs have been taken out from the Google Play and the Apple application stores. Also, YouTube erased hundreds of crypto-related recordings. This activity — which unexpectedly ended up being a misstep — shows both an extreme issue with concentrated stages and one of the primary

benefits of blockchain innovation. Mechanically, 2019 was an astonishing year. Many organizations began to embrace Blockchain as a promising innovation by creating framework for digital currencies. Many activities create sidechains, scaling arrangements, decentralized finance foundation, noncustodial capacity advances, resource tokenization, and nonmonetary applications. This speed increase of innovative work in the field gives a look into an interesting future. Standpoint It is very normal for principal developments to encounter win and fail cycles. The website blast lead to comparative promising and less promising times and furthermore came about in overstated costs and expanded short-run assumptions. Notwithstanding, over the long haul, the web became quite possibly of the most earth shattering advancement and the establishment for new mechanical leap forwards that could never have been conceivable in any case. Thusly, value conversation won't be the focal point of this book. We will rather zero in on a mechanical what's more, monetary examination and furnish the peruser with the devices to comprehend a innovation that might turn out to be similarly just about as pivotal as the web.

CHAPTER IV

More Than Money

Universe of Warcraft is among the best computer games ever, with north of 12 million paying players at its pinnacle. In 2010, as a feature of its normal finetuning of the game, the designer debilitated a well known assault for the warlock class. It ended up being a game changing choice. Vitalik Buterin, a splendid Canadian secondary school understudy, was among the bad-to-the-bone players appalled by the move. Seeing it to act as an illustration of the "detestations incorporated administrations can bring," he quit the game and cast about for another thing to invest his energy in. He tracked down Bitcoin. Despite the fact that he was immediately snared, Buterin thought advanced money was excessively restricting. As he reviewed, "I circumvented the world, investigated numerous crypto projects, lastly understood that they were really quite concerned about unambiguous applications and not being adequately general." So at age 19, he made plans to complete the insurgency that Satoshi Nakamoto started. Buterin might well have succeeded. Ethereum, the venture he started, turned into the most unmistakable appearance of the blockchain's subsequent demonstration. This new stage would put the odd, outcast innovation on the front pages of significant papers and make it a noticeable subject for commanders of industry, titans of money, and heads of government. It would up the ante significantly, in both positive and negative ways. A cryptographic money that can be used to purchase a pizza, as bitcoin was in 2010, is a great accomplishment, yet, conveyed records that help multibillion dollar (or maybe sometime in the future multitrillion dollar) worldwide business biological systems are something completely different. Bitcoin started off the blockchain period as a verifiable matter. Notwithstanding, it addresses only one corner of the significant calculated space. The normal term incorporating the bigger group of approaches is "conveyed record." Bitcoin can be perceived as the principal generally embraced appropriated record framework. You might accept that you sent me five bitcoin out of the twenty you initially held, yet how would I follow along? Furthermore, how do I have any idea that is truly bitcoin, and that you got it from a real exchange? Moving significant resources requires a settled after recording instrument. Seeing Bitcoin and its offspring in this manner assists with explaining why their true capacity is so a lot more prominent than computerized cash. A record is a record of records. Maybe the most recognizable records are those utilized for twofold passage accounting, the groundwork of bookkeeping. In any case, records are not restricted to recording charges and credits for corporate accounting reports. Housing markets couldn't exist without land title libraries. A majority rules system requires records for counting votes. Copyright depends on both public and confidential records following the enlistment and task of freedoms. The cutting edge firm relies upon records for its financials, however for the connections among its inside specialists and outer accomplices, too as its inventory network, administrative center, and client confronting exercises. Powerful sociologists, for example, Max Weber and Werner Sombart contended that doubleentry accounting was the underpinning of present day free enterprise. In Weber's words, "the most broad presupposition for the presence of this presentday free enterprise is that of reasonable capital book keeping. "4 Records contain the fundamental framework for monitoring things. By laying out a solid record of proprietorship and resource streams, they reinforce property privileges. They additionally permit such privileges to be partitioned what's more, executed around, through progressively complex authoritative arrangements. Guidelines like Proper accounting rules (GAAP) can be embraced on top of the records, and afterward reviewing/revealing necessities, inward controls, and more can be additionally layered on top. As recordkeeping moved from paper records to independent PCs to advanced networks, the extent of records expanded. In the advanced world, with huge quantities of monetary exchanges and similarly huge development of different resources all over the planet, records are a higher priority than at any other time. Blockchain frameworks are organizations of records. The beginning up Wave was evidently the first to utilize "Web of Significant worth" for this bigger phenomenon. It catches that similarly as the Web connected networks for the trade of data, blockchain will trade significant resources. Cash is only the first such resource. A jewel neckband, portions of stock, a brand name, and tickets to a show are resources with esteem. Furthermore, in this day and age, information has esteem too. Google assembled one of the world's most productive organizations on its capacity to gather, investigate, and influence information into significant administrations. Appropriated records hold out the chance of comparably strong information accumulation, however without the drawbacks of incorporated control. Bitcoin, to some degree at first, was restricted to

a solitary capability: digital money installment exchanges. Ethereum addressed a jump to dynamic records that can, in principle, support any application that can be coded in programming. In such
a climate, additionally, stages can be independent from applications. A bookkeeping sheet is both a record and the product application carrying out that record. A distributed computing stage, for example, Amazon Web Administrations, not with standing, is particular from applications and administrations that work on top of it. In the equivalent way, the Bitcoin network stage was initially indistinct from the bitcoin installment cash, however open blockchain networks are establishments for a scope of decentralized applications (Dapps). As far back as 2010, Satoshi Nakamoto and other Bitcoin designers estimated in web-based conversations about utilizing blockchain innovation in regions past advanced cash.6 Namecoin, the underlying framework in light of those discussions, makes Web area name enrollment restriction safe in the same way that Bitcoin accomplishes for installments. It sent off in 2011 as the principal fork of the Bitcoin codebase.7 There are likewise ways of making new cryptographic forms of money or more unique usefulness while proceeding to record data on the Bitcoin record. Bitcoin permits regions down to 100 millionth of a coin (called a "Satoshi"). A useless fragment of a coin can be labeled or "shaded" to address another resource, even an undeniable option coin. There are likewise processes called "consolidate mining" and "fixed sidechains," under which a cryptographic money organization can piggyback onto Bitcoin's verification of work to approve its transactions.9 These methodologies, in actuality, get the trust that Bitcoin's agreement network creates for new purposes.

As certain groups tried to expand on top of the Bitcoin record, others imagined new cryptographic money frameworks made without any preparation. These "Bitcoin 2.0" networks commonly veered from Bitcoin's two plan objectives: They tended to some different option from installments, they loosened up the prerequisite that no third parties be relied upon, or both. Swell sent off in 2012. It maintained Bitcoin's attention on installments, however it consolidated a set number of confided in approval hubs to serve controlled banks keen on more effectively getting cash across borders. The broadly useful Ethereum network became functional in 2015.10 Other digital currency stages are pushing on various aspects. For instance, Monero, Run, and ZCash offer digital currencies with more grounded obscurity assurance than Bitcoin. Furthermore, both NEO and Qtum are situating themselves as the "blockchain of Asia," exploiting areas of strength for the interest in digital forms of money in that area of the planet. Today, there are two or three dozen other public blockchain networks in activity. Also, that is only a glimpse of something larger. Actually 2017, there were more than 80,000 blockchain-situated projects on the open-source programming vault Github.11 One site recorded in excess of 1,500 digital money tokens accessible as of April 2018, for the most part running on top of Ethereum or other essential agreement platforms.12 These tokens serve a wide assortment of capabilities. For instance, the Fundamental Consideration Token (BAT) gave by the beginning up Bold is utilized to repay clients for review designated promotions. The Filecoin token related with Entomb Planetary Record Framework (IPFS) redresses the individuals who share hard drive space for dispersed distributed storage. Numerai repays information researchers who propose fruitful calculations that it would be able set to deal with its mutual funds. Acquire.com is an interpersonal organization that pays clients in tokens for following through with responsibilities, for example, answering messages or filling out surveys.13 Alleged Bitcoin maximalists contend that Bitcoin's solid security — due to its lengthy history and more prominent handling power dedicated to mining — will make it the best stage for all digital money based exercises. They consider interest in different stages to be an interruption. A restricting group sees Bitcoin as the confirmation of idea for digital currencies or conveyed record advancements, which will before long be abandoned as different stages outperform its usefulness. One of the major questions is versatility. As action has expanded, throughput on the Bitcoin network has eased back. Those wishing to put through exchanges have been compelled to connect significant charges to boost diggers to rapidly deal with them. In Satoshi Nakamoto's unique plan, exchange expenses would increase just once the Bitcoin block reward dwindled, and however in 2017, they frequently spiked to $10 or more per exchange. This made little worth installments uneconomical, killing the first center use for the cash. There are various scaling proposition for Bitcoin, including answers for handle most exchanges off the blockchain while proceeding to depend on the agreement interaction for security. The open inquiry is whether retrofitting Bitcoin checks out than changing to an organization with better versatility planned into it all along.

Chia replaces verification of work's costly calculation with verification of accessible hard drive space. Particle, a dispersed Web of Things (IoT) framework for controlling organization associated gadgets, gets rid of the blockchain information structure completely for what it calls a "tangle," which seemingly turns out better for countless hubs with restricted processing power.16 These and different strategies guarantee significantly further developed execution and security contrasted with more-laid out arrangements. A few have great specialized sponsorship, like Algorand's Silvio Micali, a conspicuous MIT cryptographer, what's more, Chia's Bram Cohen, who made the generally utilized BitTorrent record sharing convention. Regardless of their assortment, this large number of approaches are conspicuous relatives of Bitcoin. They produce a reliable normal truth in an organization with no focal control or intermediation. None of the more up to date frameworks yet has this present reality approval and engineer foothold of Bitcoin and Ethereum.

Notwithstanding, it is too soon to reach authoritative decisions about which approaches will win. Times of serious trial and error definitely produce wrong turns and impasses alongside advancement developments. The most striking reality is the complexity and variety of advancement around blockchain-related agreement innovations. Significantly seriously striking, this explosion of movement isn't restricted to new companies. It has developed to incorporate a portion of the world's most remarkable organizations.

The Bitcoin network is the foundation of the Bitcoin framework. It associates the person network members and permits them to transfer exchanges and blocks. It is consequently significant to the framework's conditional limit. Bitcoin is a shared organization (figure 3.1a). As opposed to incorporated networks (figure 3.1b), in the Bitcoin network no member plays a favored part. The members normally have countless associations, and new associations can be laid out between any two members. Each member can hold a neighborhood duplicate of the Bitcoin blockchain, check the authenticity of exchanges, and send these to other network members. This grants correspondence and information stockpiling to work in the nonattendance of a focal party. The decentralized engineering makes distributed networks especially impervious to assaults and disappointments. While in a unified organization the disappointment of a focal hub can have deadly outcomes and can at times prompt information misfortune or a total breakdown of correspondence, in a shared organization each member can be supplanted. Disappointments are generally handily taken care of by other organization members, privately lost information is reestablished, also, correspondence is kept up with on elective association ways. In this regard, decentralized frameworks are not subject to individual hubs. Their design forestalls a singular member from involving a framework important position and subsequently makes them more strong.

According to an administrative point of view, decentralization likewise gives a networkwith a certain resistance. It is extremely challenging to direct the entire organization because of the shortfall of focal resources. Whenever a hub is shut, one can undoubtedly make a new one.2 Likewise, guideline doesn't have a similar level of desperation in decentralized frameworks. Unified networks depend on members' confidence in a focal power. This trust can be mishandled by controlling the midway put away information. Controls in their own advantage or to serve a client are similarly possible. Among the present frameworks, it is expected that a blend of notoriety impacts, control components, furthermore, fines gives the proper motivators and urges focal specialists to take part in long haul collaboration. In this regard, guidelines of unified frameworks are vital. In decentralized networks reputational impacts are basically nonexistent, attributable to the unique organization geography and the pseudonymity of the members. The organization

members will possibly conform to the agreement convention in the event that it is to their greatest advantage. One outcome of this is that each member needs to consider that their friends may be transferring misleading data. In part 4, we will consider the techniques that permit network members to confirm the exactness of the (exchange) messages they get. To a limited extent I of this book, we utilized the term network member as an umbrella term, without recognizing the different capabilities these members might do. In particular, there are three fundamental capabilities: the confirmation capability, the wallet capability, and the mining capability. From this point forward, we will utilize the term network hub for a member who performs somewhere around one of the three capabilities. Check capability. The check capability covers every one of the exercises that are essential so that network members can take part in the organization all alone and check all exchanges freely. Specifically, members check exchange messages, store these messages locally, and forward them to other organization members. The confirmation capability requires a member to keep a duplicate of the Bitcoin blockchain what's more, to confirm the legitimacy of the relative multitude of blocks of the chain. The confirmation capability moreover works with the trading of blocks. Network hubs who have a confirmation capability are known as full hubs. Wallet capability. A wallet gives safe capacity to private keys andmonitors and makes due a hub's very own Bitcoin balance.Wallets are created for end clients and typically give a graphical UI that empowers Bitcoin units to be gotten and sent without any problem. Moreover, numerous wallets offer discretionary security systems to work on the security of the confidential keys.

Mining capability. Hubs that have a mining capability partake effectively in creating new blocks and add to the augmentation of the Bitcoin blockchain. Another organization hub is made when a client introduces a Bitcoin client on his PC also, starts to trade data with other organization members. Most clients are open source, and clients are allowed to look over a scope of programming bundles. Hypothetically, a client could likewise foster his own client and allow it to speak with the organization. However long the product bundles are consistent with Bitcoin's correspondence convention, they can be utilized to make new hubs and trade data. The most famous client is known as Bitcoin Center. Bitcoin Center contains the full reach of capabilities. The product makes a full hub and can be controlled through a graphical client interface or through the order line. Bitcoin Center keeps a neighborhood duplicate of the Bitcoin blockchain. The client checks and transfers the exchanges and blocks. Furthermore, Bitcoin Center incorporates a wallet and a straightforward mining application. It accordingly gives each of the three capabilities. Bitcoin Center is a openly downloadable programming.

The quantity of full hubs not the slightest bit mirrors the quantity of Bitcoin clients. The increment in the size of the Bitcoin blockchain and the expansion in the quantity of exchanges has prompted a developing rundown of necessities with respect to a full hub's equipment and web particulars. For this reason numerous clients rule against working a full hub themselves and on second thought depend on different members who work a full hub. A rethought approval implies, for instance, that the Bitcoin blockchain doesn't should be downloaded and continually refreshed. The asset investment funds can be especially fascinating for clients on cell phones, where memory is normally scant and transfer speed restricted. Restricted network investment offers the opportunities for the straightforward mix of clients who could somehow or another pass on the Bitcoin organization. Simultaneously, notwithstanding, the relinquishment of the confirmation capability produces conditions. The Bitcoin framework offers each organization member the chance of autonomously confirming the authenticity of all exchanges remembered for the Bitcoin blockchain. In the event that an organization member forgoes this choice, he consequently loses part of his freedom and should put a specific measure of confidence in his data sources. Brought together subnetworks show the most elevated type of reliance. The members are simply by implication associated with the Bitcoin organization and depend solely on the data what's more, interchanges channel of a particular hub. Figure 3.5 shows two brought together subnetworks.

Clients that are associated with a concentrated subnetwork can practice the wallet capability without the requirement for direct admittance to the Bitcoin organization. The focal hub is utilized as an intermediary server, which can be counseled intermittently to check the Bitcoin adjusts of the client's locations. Also, exchange messages are sent to the focal hub and in this way by implication handed-off to the Bitcoin organization. An association with an incorporated subnetwork can be considerably more helpful for a client since he has just to introduce a light client or to deal with his Bitcoin adjusts through a web application. The subsequent conditions are not really observable under typical activities. Nonetheless, a focal hub would be able to either keep specific data from the members or not transfer their exchanges to the remainder of the organization and subsequently block them. This should be possible purposefully or can occur as an outcome of specialized issues. In this regard, brought together subnetworks lose a huge piece of the power properties of a distributed organization and bring new weaknesses into the framework. By and large, incorporated subnetworks are likewise joined by guardianship administrations. In such connections, the proprietor moves unlimited authority of his Bitcoin units to the focal hub. He doesn't hold a confidential key for the comparing balance yet as it were has a client account on the specialist co-op's foundation, with which he can demand the conveyance of his Bitcoin units. The genuine Bitcoin exchange is started by the focal hub. In such a relationship, the client just gets an IOU promising to convey the Bitcoin units on demand. This is equivalent to credit cash, for which the worth of the commitment relies upon the financial soundness of the backer (see segment 1.4.2). SPV clients work with the utilization of the wallet capability without it being important to store a full duplicate of the Bitcoin blockchain locally. Instead of circuitous organization members who are attached to a focal hub, SPV hubs have direct admittance to the Bitcoin network. The necessary information are obtained by different hubs and can be to some extent confirmed. The variety of information sources and the chance of somewhat checking the got information give the SPV hub more noteworthy security and freedom than an association with a brought together subnetwork.

A SPV hub holds just a little piece of the blocks — the purported block header. In addition to other things, the block header incorporates the recognizable proof number that depends on the exchanges included however not the exchanges themselves.5 Thus, SPV clients require something like a thousandth of the stockpiling limit of full hubs. An SPV client requirements to store just eighty bytes for each block. All the more critically, this sum stays unaltered no matter what the quantity of exchanges included, coming about in a direct development way even with a huge expansion in clients and exchanges. Full hubs utilize the block level to check an exchange. To guarantee that the Bitcoin unit (unspent exchange yield) referred to in an exchange has not as of now been utilized, the full hubs check the total Bitcoin blockchain.6 SPV hubs rather utilize a heuristic in light of the block profundity — that is, the quantity of affirmations that got an exchange. In the event that the block is referred to by a specific number of extra blocks (generally six), SPV hubs respect the exchanges contained in it as legitimate. Because of the great computational assets expected to make these resulting blocks and the different sources utilized to get the data, the likelihood of a control endeavor is exceptionally low. SPVs source data by specifically questioning individual exchanges. This makes two issues. To begin with, SPV hubs can check whether a got exchange really has a place with a block; be that as it may, they don't know whether they are being denied data or whether another, potentially contending exchange exists.

Second, data social event can prompt protection issues. On the off chance that a SPV hub inquires just for exchanges regarding its own public keys (or Bitcoin addresses), the different hubs will actually want to interface these pen names its IP address and make a unmistakable client profile. As a countermeasure, the SPV hub could demand an enormous sum of extra information. In any case, the huge volume of information would sabotage the first reason for carrying out the SPV client. To neutralize the subsequent issue, exchanges are normally questioned by means of purported blossom channels. Blossom channels indicate a hunt demand utilizing hash capabilities (see segment 4.2). The SPV hub sends a solicitation for exchanges that match a specific pursuit design later applying different hash capabilities. The accuracy can shift as indicated by prerequisites. There is as yet a compromise among security and information volume. Misleading positive outcomes are conceivable or on the other hand even attractive as a result of the probabilistic idea of the framework. Misleading negative results are unrealistic. In the event that an exchange is dismissed by the channel, it is superfluous for the SPV client. Sprout channels effectively disguise the pursuit inquiries by SPV hubs. Due to the idea of the hash capability, it is a lot harder to distinguish the example behind the inquiry. The thought started with a scholarly paper by Bloom[40] and was formalized by BIP0037[111] for the Bitcoin framework. Bitcoin mining is much of the time performed mutually by enormous gatherings, alluded to as mining pools. Exemplary performance mining requires the activity of a full hub. Pool mining, in any case, doesn't. Ordinarily just the pool administrator holds a duplicate of the Bitcoin blockchain and conveys the necessary data to the pool individuals similarly as a unified subnetwork. Pool mining is thusly a significant supporter of the decrease in the quantity of full hubs and energizes worry about centralization infringing on the Bitcoin framework. The reason for the Bitcoin network is to take into consideration the trading of data. For this data to be handled by different clients, correspondence should happen in a normalized structure. No client can be compelled to agree with these principles. The correspondence convention only portrays the designing of the data. If a hub needs to speak with different hubs, it is consequently to its greatest advantage to stick to this arrangement. For the Bitcoin organization, the trading of blocks and exchanges is fundamentally important. Messages that don't straightforwardly serve the trading of this kind of data play an optional job. At the point when the client programming is initially begun, it endures a few hours downloading, checking, also, ordering every one of the blocks of the Bitcoin blockchain. The main block, the beginning block, is coordinated into the client programming on conveyance. All resulting blocks need to be obtained from different hubs and confirmed by the client programming.

The volume of information contained in the Bitcoin blockchain was roughly 205 gigabytes (GB) at the end of 2019. Each block should be downloaded and confirmed just a single time. Long stacking times happen provided that the client needs to get up to speed with countless blocks; that is, during the underlying establishment of the client programming or on the other hand in the event that the hub was not associated with the organization for quite a while. The examination between two duplicates of the Bitcoin blockchain happens by means of the shared trade of getblocks messages. These messages contain the ID number of the most current block in the nearby chain. Assuming the two chains are same, no blocks should be traded. Be that as it may, in the event that one of the two hubs gets a getblocks message with a recognizable proof number that doesn't relate to the last block of the nearby chain, it will attempt to find the block with this ID number inside the neighborhood chain and send an inv (stock) message with the ID numbers of the replacements of this block.

The hub that gets the inv message, then, at that point, has the likelihood to demand the particular blocks utilizing getdata messages. Shows the informing history between the two hubs while sending blocks. This guideline is utilized to keep a hub from getting block information that it as of now has. Every hub can autonomously conclude which information it needs to demand from which hubs. At the point when a hub gets a block, he freely looks at the legitimacy of the exchanges that it contains and checks that the exchanges reference just beforehand unspent exchange yields (UTXO) and were started by the proprietor. The hub additionally looks at the reference to the old block and analyzes the ongoing block's distinguishing proof number to decide if itmeets the edge esteem standard. Each hub can in this manner obviously decide if a block satisfies the different agreement conditions. If and provided that all checks are passed, the hub will incorporate the block into his rendition of the blockchain.

Exchange messages are installment arranges that hubs can confirm, hand-off, and process. We will take a gander at the construction and the confirmation of an exchange message in segment. In the current segment, we center around how exchange messages are transferred. The strategy for trading exchange messages is basically the same as that utilized for blocks. The inv messages can on the other hand incorporate exchange ID numbers. Assuming a hub gets an inv message that contains an obscure exchange ID number, the hub can comparatively utilize a getdata message to demand the exchange. The genuine transmission of the exchange information is in this way made utilizing a tx message. The informing history between the two hubs while sending exchanges. On the off chance that a hub gets a mentioned tx message, it will initially look at it and forward as it were assuming the approval is effective. The approval is performed utilizing predefined opening conditions and marks, which we will consider exhaustively in segment 4.5. If approval falls flat, the exchange will be disposed of. This shields the organization from particular sorts of DoS assaults, which make information transmissions seize up by flooding the assistance with an enormous number of invalid exchanges. Nonetheless, assuming that the approval is fruitful, memory, the purported mempool, what's more, proposed to different hubs as a feature of the inv message. Under particular conditions, hubs might have a motivator not to advance exchange messages. In the event that the exchange expenses are a significant piece of the prize, excavators can build their own normal result by keeping information. This issue can undoubtedly be helped by the initiator of the exchange by sending it to a few free mining hubs. As to the correspondence of blocks, a comparative issue can happen. In some cases it is beneficial for aminer (mining pool) to keep a block with a substantial distinguishing proof number mystery and work solely on the longest form of the blockchain. Albeit the digger in this way faces the gamble that another digger could go after his ongoing prize, he can additionally accordingly keep his rivals from dealing with the longest rendition of the chain and in this way guarantee that they squander a specific extent of their computational assets. Since the normal result for mining is relative to the complete computational assets of every one of the diggers, holding a substantial block can expand the normal result of an excavator. This peculiarity is known as egotistical mining. The maintenance of blocks represents a far more prominent issue than the maintenance of exchanges. There are different methodologies that moderate this issue by guaranteeing it just becomes advantageous to hold new blocks when the excavator has around 33% of the entirety organization's computational assets.

In principle, anybody can work a full hub on the Bitcoin organization, mine digital money, what's more, confirm exchanges. It is basically impossible to tell on the organization itself in the event that a member is a Fortune 500 organization or a needed worldwide criminal.17 No administration can control the items in the Bitcoin blockchain since it is appropriated among numerous PCs all over the planet running open-source programming. It would continue to run regardless of whether the greater part of them were taken disconnected. No confidential entertainer can drive the organization to move in a specific bearing but in the impossible occasion that it controls a larger part of mining power. Everybody has a similar admittance to the organization and a similar full perceivability into earlier exchanges. This decentralization includes some major disadvantages. One sort of cost connects with execution. Broadcasting all exchanges to all organize hubs makes a tremendous measure of above contrasted with customary information bases. Another connects with utilization. For specific applications and members, totally open access and full perceivability are nonstarters. In controlled ventures, for instance, there may be legitimate prerequisites to know the personality of counterparties. There may likewise be administrative or legally binding necessities to keep the subtleties of specific exchanges private. Furthermore, in Europe, the Overall Information Security Guideline (GDPR) commands an option to be forgotten for individual information, which commits information processors to eradicate specific data upon request.18 This, as well as the entire GDPR system of data freedoms, will be challenging to square with the irreversible exchange records of public blockchain networks.19 These expenses may be worth the effort to accomplish solid control opposition and cryptoeconomic security, basically for some utilization cases. What's more, they are probably going to drop over the long haul with the presence of new advancements to work on the exhibition of blockchain networks. Enormous classes of expected circulated record clients, notwithstanding, are eager to exchange a restricted level of decentralization for proficiency. Bitcoin revived interest in Byzantine Issue Open minded (BFT) calculations other than evidence of work. This prompted the improvement of another class of appropriated records. They are as yet decentralized, in that no element controls the network. Nonetheless, just those checked entertainers with consent from a planning body can approve exchanges, propose new ones, or now and again indeed, even view the record. Hyperledger chief Brian Behlendorf calls this idea "least suitable centralization."20 The essential adopters of this way to deal with blockchain are large companies all over the planet. The significant programming and administrations firms for those ventures, like IBM, Microsoft, PWC, Prophet, and HPE, have additionally gotten on board with that fad. A large number of the things that ventures might want to do with conveyed record frameworks include somewhat little organizations of recognized players. A gathering of promoters and distributers trying to diminish internet publicizing misrepresentation, for model, presumably needn't bother with a way for totally mysterious gatherings to take an interest. In such consortium settings, a significant number of the advantages of blockchainbased frameworks can be accomplished through other conveyed record structures that permit just those with consent to get to the network.21 These are alluded to as "permissioned," "private," or "consortium" records. The main two associations pushing the improvement of permissioned networks are Hyperledger and R3.22 Hyperledger deals with a set-up of conveyed record bundles offering various functionalities, most prominently Hyperledger Texture, in view of starting work by IBM. Its answers are intended to be measured. A permissioned organization could connect Hyperledger Tunnel's brilliant agreement execution motor or Hyperledger Indy's client controlled personality module, or utilize another arrangement. They can likewise trade out various agreement instruments relying upon their requirements. Hyperledger is a task of the philanthropic Linux Establishment, which works to normalize open-source advances and make associations between undertakings and designers. Behlendorf, its chief, is a prominent Web and opensource technologist who made Apache, the main web server programming, prior to working with the Obama White House, the World Financial Discussion, also, Paypal fellow benefactor Peter Thiel's funding firm. R3 is a for-benefit firm that works a consortium of more than eighty

significant ventures, including numerous conspicuous monetary administrations organizations. 23 R3's Corda stage utilizes appropriated record innovation to make due arrangements between monetary establishments, including money, protections, or subordinates. As R3's Richard Gendal Brown made sense of in a blog entry: The monetary business is basically characterized by the arrangements that exist between its organizations and these organizations share a typical issue: the understanding is ordinarily recorded by the two players, in various frameworks, and extremely enormous sums of cost are made by the need fix things when these various frameworks end up accepting different things.24 Corda utilizes a circulated record to keep a common record of the web of monetary arrangements among banks. Since it is intended to enhance the ongoing legitimate construction, just distinguished establishments can take part in the network. The information structure for recording exchanges is a standard social data set instead of a blockchain, and the agreement framework is based on a more customary BFT calculation. The framework can expressly welcome controllers, who can work what Corda terms "administrative spectator hubs" with admittance to ongoing data about exchanges, into the interaction. Permissioned organizations, for example, Corda and Hyperledger Texture for the most part needn't bother with evidence of work since they keep a lingering level of confidence in the character of organization members. This permits them to stay away from the expensive and limit restricting mining process. The amount of an advantage this is relies upon whether the permissioned records can keep up with adequate security and control obstruction, and whether the troubles related with verification of work are mitigated after some time through specialized progresses. These undertakings additionally do not need a devoted cryptographic money token on the grounds that their motivation is simply to help circulated record applications. Swell consolidates a permissioned network with a money, XRP, that can be exchanged yet isn't made through public mining. There is something of a strict conflict between defenders of public and permissioned records. Supporters of public organizations like Bitcoin and Ethereum contend that permissioned networks are basically data sets. In as much as somebody should be relied upon, contends Association Square Endeavors accomplice Albert Wenger, you are fundamentally important for the status quo.25 A disseminated record could offer some steady execution upgrades, however it will not change the design of enterprises or open the entryway for sensational development. As a matter of fact, the contention goes that in light of the fact that the consortium controls access, permissioned records could really support the force of occupants. Some on the public organization side of the contention say that permissioned networks shouldn't be essential for a similar discussion. At any rate, they ought not be lethargically named blockchains when, as on account of R3, they do not even store information in that frame of mind of blocks. On the opposite side, permissioned network advocates express that there is a universe of contrast between customary information base innovation and dispersed records. Data sets by and large expect that all hubs will be controlled by a confided in entertainer — ordinarily inside a similar organization. Ordinary data sets can be circulated and synchronized across different machines. In any case, those synchronization calculations are intended to prepare for machines crashing, not machines denouncing any kind of authority and attempting to sabotage the network.26 Disseminated records, paradoxically, expect that hubs are worked by free parties who have little to no faith in each other and could be effectively antagonistic foes. Antony Lewis, the Singapore-based overseer of exploration at R3, depicts this as the contrast between shared information and shared control.27 Customary information bases share information. When that occurs, in any case, those that share let completely go to anything association works the information base. The administrator continuously has the specialized capacity to access or change data.

Appropriated records, then again, share control. Each party keeps up with control over its own information, regardless of whether others can see and utilize it under determined terms. There could be no other element who can abrogate that control. It isn't really that hypothetically, no customary information base could store the data living on permissioned records. No genuine data set of all time would. Bruce Pon, CEO (President) of the blockchain-arranged information base beginning up BigChainDB, portrays a model application from the auto industry. A significant provider, for example, Bosch has an information base of the relative multitude of parts it offers. It won't surrender control of that information. If vehicle producers, wholesalers, and others need access, they should work to Bosch's application programming points of interaction and maneuver information into their own data sets. Every one of them should rehash the interaction for each provider. On the off chance that there are irregularities in the information between frameworks, they should be settled.

For the following piece of the story, we return to the previous Universe of Warcraft player depicted toward the start of this section. In 2013, Vitalik Buterin exited school. Outfitted with a $100,000 Thiel Partnership, he set about to make what turned into the Ethereum project. Ethereum, and different frameworks like it, opened up the full extent of the blockchain opportunity. They did as such by additional fostering an instrument known as a "shrewd agreement." Appropriated records are dynamic, not latent. As such, the records do not just record data passed to them. They are important for an agreement framework, so they should guarantee that recorded exchanges are really finished to match the consensus.32 For Bitcoin, that implies that the framework self-upholds monetary transfers.33 I can't start an exchange promising to send you bitcoin and afterward renege; the synchronization that accommodates furthermore, finishes the exchange is essential for the interaction. This is the shrewd agreement usefulness. Both the detail of freedoms and commitments and the execution of that legally binding understanding happen through the stage. That is totally different from conventional monetary exchanges, where clearing and settlement are unmistakable cycles from the actual understanding, and questions go through the court framework. Savvy contracts transform a circulated record into a disseminated PC. One method for understanding Satoshi Nakamoto's advancement was that he addressed the issue of decentralized time-stepping. To believe that a coin was not spent two times, there should be a dependable method for following precisely when every exchange occurred.

On a decentralized organization, in any case, there is no expert clock to which each machine can synchronize. That sounds a trusted, really third party!34 And even without one, hubs would have to trust the time stamps that different hubs revealed. The verification of-work framework forces agreement on the exact request of exchanges. Hubs are concurring on what occurred, yet in what arrangement it worked out. The very agreement calculations that permit every hub to have an indistinguishable duplicate of the record, in this way, permit it to perform indistinguishable calculations, in a similar request. That gives what PC researchers call "shared express": an image of the situation with the framework all of a sudden. As indicated by Adam Krellenstein, fellow benefactor of the shrewd agreement new businesses Symbiont and Counterparty, blockchain networks are the main genuine world frameworks to accomplish shared state with practically no confided in focal authority.35 That opens up a universe of potential outcomes. Presently disseminated records are a method for doing basically anything that PCs can do, however in a decentralized way. Brilliant contracts capability as programming programs that execute on a blockchain.36 Scratch Szabo fostered shrewd agreements during the 1990s, well before Bitcoin existed.37 His representation was the unassuming candy machine. A candy machine completely executes a legally binding understanding by taking in cash and apportioning items. It additionally gives adequate security to make penetrating the agreement — breaking into the machine — unbeneficial. For all useful purposes, the machine is the total of the authoritative climate. It needs no human mediation, either to play out the agreement or to resolve debates in court. Until Bitcoin, there were not many viable uses of these thoughts. Distributing machines function as proto-shrewd agreements since they sell things of low worth, work eye to eye, and take cash38 (a conveyor instrument). Dispersed records made it conceivable to execute comparable game plans carefully, across networks, for any sort of resource or understanding, with practically no confided in entertainer. For model, protection arrangements, home loans, wills, and programming licenses are all exchanges that today require human intermediation, yet might possibly be computerized through brilliant agreements. Indeed, even after Bitcoin acquired strength, however, it required quite a while for powerful shrewd agreement stages to be presented.

The Bitcoin convention was planned unequivocally for a money, so it as it were required the usefulness important to help monetary exchanges.

Adding more extravagant programming abilities to blockchain exchanges adds security chances and different intricacies. The more you can do with a softwarebased framework, the more open doors for bugs, exploits, and hacks. Bitcoin likewise comes up short on portrayal of shared state as records, which determine digital money property without warning. All things being equal, it utilizes a configuration called "unspent exchange yield (UTXO)." The bitcoin related with a private

key should be added up to time from past sending and getting exchanges. UTXO is in fact easier for advanced cash, yet it makes it harder to work universally useful savvy contracts. Defeating these limits was the objective of Ethereum, the most conspicuous savvy contract platform.39 Ethereum offers a Turing-complete programming language, truly intending that in principle, any application that sudden spikes in demand for a customary PC can be executed on the disseminated record through its agreement organization. 40 Ethereum is planned as a total savvy contract stage, including advancement apparatuses. It makes it generally simple to code new sorts of uses on top, similarly as the web and different programming apparatuses like application servers were the establishment for Google, Amazon, and eBay. How precisely shrewd agreement innovation will be embraced is an open inquiry. Szabo's 1997 paper, for instance, imagined a brilliant vehicle rent.

If the driver neglected to make regularly scheduled installments, the vehicle would consequently be delivered inoperable and control of the keys returned to the bank. Exactly the same thing would happen toward the finish of the rent term, except if the understanding was a rent to

buy, in which case the bank's entrance would shut down upon full installment. Such a framework would be intended to smooth implementation of a natural class of understanding. As will be talked about in part 6, however, it could likewise create new issues when the computerized implementation goes excessively far.

Shrewd agreements can likewise empower completely new sorts of game plans. Maybe the best early illustration of an application based on Ethereum is CryptoKitties, a game that sent off in late 2017 and immediately became one of the greatest wellsprings of traffic on the network.41 The application creates

novel advanced collectibles as animation little cats. The little cats, each of which is really a cryptographic money token executing brilliant agreements, can be reproduced with one another to make novel posterity arbitrarily.

A portion of these are very interesting. Something like one offered to a gatherer for more than $100,000 in digital money. In spite of the fact that CryptoKitties is possible a fleeting craze, it recommends the variety of purposes for brilliant agreements. Advanced resources that can't be copied be that as it may, can be sold and changed could have serious applications in finance also, other business spaces. What buterin would call a broadly useful registering stage on similar establishments as Bitcoin pulled in huge energy very quickly later the Ethereum whitepaper was delivered in late 2013. Advancement started in 2014 and was in the end formalized under a Swiss establishment. Ethereum utilized the then-novel methodology, presently known as an underlying coin offering, of selling pre-functional tokens to raise financing. Today, there are organizations of Ethereum engineers all over the planet. Consensys, a Brooklyn, New York-based programming improvement studio drove by Ethereum prime supporter Joe Lubin, is hatching many Ethereum-based projects, a few of which have proactively turned out as free organizations. And then some than 200 associations, including Microsoft, JPMorgan, the public authority of India, Intel, Cisco, and Mastercard, are individuals from the Undertaking Ethereum Collusion, a gathering shaped to advance Ethereum reception among laid out businesses.42 Ethereum has its own local cryptographic money, called "ether." It is currently the second most important, after bitcoin. In any case, ether's main role isn't to act as a speculation vehicle or installment component. It is the main way to buy an inside, nontradable asset in the Ethereum framework, called "gas." Gas purchases handling cycles on the Ethereum organization. A more confounded shrewd agreement, requiring more calculation, costs more gas. What's more, there is a hard breaking point on how much gas that any Ethereum shrewd agreement can exhaust. Ethereum adopted this strategy for two reasons. In the first place, calculation is exorbitant. In the Ethereum organization, as a public blockchain framework, each confirmation hub processes each brilliant contract.43 The framework is hard proportional, particularly in the event that brilliant agreement engineers are not miserly in that frame of mind of calculation. It would rapidly obstruct in the event that anybody could send off thousands of shrewd agreements with no expense. Second, shrewd agreements are programs.

CHAPTER V

Transactions Transparency

In this section, we will take a gander at how Bitcoin units can be relegated to an individual and which standards of science empower a decentralized approval of an exchange's authenticity. We present pen names develop the important cryptographic establishments. We present the different exchange types as well as the particular conditions that must be satisfied for Bitcoin units to be sent. Inferable from the decentralized design of the Bitcoin organization, it is unimaginable tomanage Bitcoin adjusts and access privileges in a conventional way. There is no focal power that is answerable for opening records, recording proprietors' very own subtleties, and approving resulting access. Hence, decentralization makes it incredibly troublesome to inspect the authenticity of possession claims. The utilization of genuine characters as private names and individual subtleties is not one or the other achievable nor attractive in the Bitcoin framework. It isn't attractive since, supposing that Bitcoin addresses were enlisted under private names, partner all future conceivable exchanges to people. Data about compensation installments, buy inclinations, also, privately invested money would be available to everybody. It isn't doable in light of the fact that in a decentralized framework it is difficult to give verification of character similarly as in
the conventional monetary framework.

The Bitcoin framework utilizes nom de plumes of genuine characters to ensure the authenticity of exchanges. A nom de plume arrangement in a decentralized framework expects that the accompanying circumstances are met:

1. Members should have the option to make their own pen names the help of a focal party.
2. No two nom de plumes cross-over. Possession cases to the nom de plumes be freely undeniable so that admittance to the particular Bitcoin adjusts can be limited. Bitcoin fulfills these circumstances by utilizing sets of cryptographic keys. A couple comprises of a private and a public key. The public key (or the Bitcoin address got from it) acts as a pen name addresses the character of the particular member yet can't be handily connected to an individual (point 1).1 by and by, the quantity of nom de plumes so

huge that the likelihood of two people picking a similar nom de plume irrelevant (point 2). The confidential key must continuously stay in the select ownership of the individual who produced the pen name subsequently gives confirmation that the proprietor of the individual nom de plume approved to utilize it (point 3). To make a key pair, an individual should choose indiscriminately a component from an unfathomably huge arrangement of numbers which goes from 1 to 115, 792, 089, 237, 316, 195, 423, 570, 985, 008, 687, 907, 852, 837, 564, 279, 074, 904, 382, 605, 163, 141, 518, 161, 494, 336; that is, among 1 and a 78 digit number.2 The chose number fills in as a private key and can be in this manner used to give confirmation of possession.

As displayed in figure 4.1, the public key is gotten from the confidential key. It is determined by increasing a usually known base point G of the elliptic bend by the beforehand chosen private key kprv (see area 4.3.4). Thus, the public key is a point Kpub on an elliptic bend that is addressed by a x and a y esteem. The augmentation is displayed in the recipe beneath: Kpub =kprv ∘G. It is vital that duplications in view of elliptic bends can't be inverted.3 In any case, each individual who realizes the alias then infer the relating

right of access as the confidential key. Inferable from the one-way capability, individuals can uncover their public key as a alias simultaneously holding restrictive information on their confidential key. An individual can pick a confidential key, get a pen name it, and get a Bitcoin Many pieces of Bitcoin's usefulness depend on hash capabilities. For instance, the block recognizable proof number from segment 2.4.3 is just the hash worth of the block header. The Bitcoin address from segment 4.1.3 is a hash worth of the related public key, and, surprisingly, individual exchanges can be recognized by their hash values. In this regard, a short deviation to make sense of hash capabilities is basic. Consider hash capability H, which doles out a hash esteem h to an info m so that H(m)=h. The information isn't liable to any shape necessities and can be a person line of any length. The hash esteem h, notwithstanding, has a restricted arrangement of values and is shown as a parallel line of a specific length. The planning is deterministic. Guaranteed input m will thusly consistently prompt a similar hash an incentive for a given hash capability. Hash capabilities are not injective, so it is conceivable that various data sources might deliver the same hash esteem. Such covers are classified "impacts."A straightforward utilization of hash values are checksums. On account of the Worldwide Financial balance Number

(IBAN) in the conventional financial framework, the initial two characters after the nation code, for example, structure a hash esteem that is processed on the premise of the remainder of the record number.In the event that an individual makes a composing blunder while entering the IBAN, this checksum typically no longer matches the record number entered. The passage can in this manner be quickly distinguished as invalid, and the individual is told of the mix-up before the installment request gets communicated. For the hash capability to fill its need, it should have the accompanying two properties:

1. While attempting various data sources, all hash values ought to happen with a similar likelihood.
2. Indeed, even little changes to the info ought to cause an adjustment of the hash esteem. A hash capability with the depicted qualities will just safeguard against unplanned errors like composing botches. When the areas of use are more mind boggling and intentional control might prompt issues, it is critical to utilize cryptographic hash capabilities. With these capabilities it is difficult to create intentionally hash values with explicit attributes or prompt crashes (impact obstruction). Cryptographic hash capabilities open up new applications. Two of these applications that are of specific significance for Bitcoin are made sense of beneath.

Cryptographic hash capabilities can guarantee the honesty of the first information. This assurance works for texts of any length. For this reason, the hash worth of the info that should be safeguarded is registered and put away. Since any changes in accordance with the first input unavoidably lead to an alternate hash esteem, a change of the first information will be perceived right away. Because of the properties of the cryptographic hash capabilities, it will likewise not be feasible for an individual to intentionally create an impact; that is, to see as an elective information, which brings about a similar hash esteem. The hash worth will respond to the littlest change in a text. Indeed, even basically changing a single letter or accentuation imprint will make the hash esteem be totally unique. This can best be outlined by utilizing two instances of texts whose hash values were figured utilizing the hash capability SHA256.7 It is striking how comparable the model texts are, while their hash values are plainly altogether different Since it is preposterous to intentionally create hash values with explicit qualities, cryptographic hash capabilities can likewise act as evidence that by and large, a specific sum of computational assets were utilized to produce a hash esteem with predefined qualities.

For instance, assuming somebody needs to introduce the contributions to a hash esteem that has a 0 at the primary hexadecimal position, this individual should contribute some computational assets and attempt different data sources. On normal just every sixteenth info will prompt a hash esteem that meets this criterion.9 If the initial two positions both need to expect to be the esteem 0, the likelihood drops to (116)2. By fixing or releasing this necessity, any level of trouble can be accomplished. To keep hash values from being made available for later furthermore, utilized as confirmation for different applications, the info as a rule contains an application explicit part. To get the variety, the info likewise contains a variable part with erratic information that can be picked openly. This wellspring of variety permits different hash values to

be figured from in any case equivalent information. Cryptographic hash capabilities structure the groundwork of Bitcoin's agreement convention. In segment we have proactively utilized it to register the blocks' ID numbers. A complete conversation continues in segment.

We will presently go to marks. We will show how people in general and confidential keys are numerically connected together and how confidential keys can be utilized to demonstrate possession of a specific pen name as evidence of the genuineness and respectability of an exchange message. Since we need to dig into the fundamentals of cryptography, this segment will unavoidably be more perplexing and numerical than the remainder of the book. Nonetheless, the concentration keeps on being on conceivability, which can on occasion struggle with numerical accuracy. Subsequently, the mathematician might experience conscious improvements in these conversations.

Traditional utilizations of cryptography depend on symmetric encryption techniques. Two gatherings need to encode their correspondence and settle on a mystery key that can be utilized to encode and unscramble the messages. A similar key can consequently be utilized for corresponding correspondence. Symmetric encryption strategies have an essential limitation. For two gatherings to concur on a vital k without an outsider having the option to catch this data and consequently learn about the key, theymust at first have a solid correspondence channel through which they can trade the key. Unbalanced encryption techniques eliminate the need to utilize a solid correspondence channel. They empower an underlying key trade through channels that are possibly compromised also, can be tapped. Rather than a typical key k, each party makes its own key pair comprising of a confidential key kprv and a public key Kpub. The public key can be uncovered. Notwithstanding, the confidential key should be kept rigorously classified consistently. Key matches have the numerical property that the public key is gotten from the related private key yet might itself at any point be utilized to determine the confidential key (see figure 4.1). One more intriguing trait of these key sets is that the messages which are scrambled with one key can be unscrambled with the other key. This element works with two potential applications, as represented in figure 4.6. Mystery. Any party can utilize the public key of one more party to encode a message. Since the related confidential key is expected for decoding, the proprietor of the key pair is the as it were party ready to decode this message. For instance, in the event that an individual's charge card data is scrambled with an internet based shipper's public key, then, at that point, just that vendor can see the information. Genuineness and uprightness. On the off chance that one party scrambles a message with its own confidential key, the data can be decoded by some other party. Just the comparing public key is expected for this. This element can be utilized to guarantee the realness and respectability of a message. Decoding with a public key is just conceivable on the off chance that the message has been scrambled with the relating private key and the scrambled text has not been changed. This highlight ensures that the message was without a doubt produced by the proprietor of the vital pair (validness) and was not hence modified (trustworthiness). This cryptographic guideline is otherwise called a computerized signature. Bitcoin utilizes advanced marks to check the genuineness and trustworthiness of exchange messages.